Highlights

Highlights of GAO-12-8, a report to the Chairman, Subcommittee on Immigration, Refugees, and Border Security, Committee on the Judiciary, United States Senate

November 2011

CYBERSECURITY HUMAN CAPITAL

Initiatives Need Better Planning and Coordination

Why GAO Did This Study

Threats to federal information technology (IT) infrastructure and systems continue to grow in number and sophistication. The ability to make federal IT infrastructure and systems secure depends on the knowledge, skills, and abilities of the federal and contractor workforce that implements and maintains these systems.

In light of the importance of recruiting and retaining cybersecurity personnel, GAO was asked to assess (1) the extent to which federal agencies have implemented and established workforce planning practices for cybersecurity personnel and (2) the status of and plans for governmentwide cybersecurity workforce initiatives.

GAO evaluated eight federal agencies with the highest IT budgets to determine their use of workforce planning practices for cybersecurity staff by analyzing plans, performance measures, and other information. GAO also reviewed plans and programs at agencies with responsibility for governmentwide cybersecurity workforce initiatives.

What GAO Recommends

GAO is making recommendations to enhance individual agency cybersecurity workforce planning activities and to address governmentwide cybersecurity workforce challenges through better planning, coordination, and evaluation of governmentwide activities. Agencies concurred with the majority of GAO's recommendations and outlined steps to address them. Two agencies did not provide comments on the report.

View GAO-12-8 or key components. For more information, contact Gregory C. Wilshusen at (202) 512-6244 or wilshuseng@gao.gov or Valerie C. Melvin at (202) 512-6304 or melvinv@gao.gov.

What GAO Found

Federal agencies have taken varied steps to implement workforce planning practices for cybersecurity personnel. Five of eight agencies, including the largest, the Department of Defense, have established cybersecurity workforce plans or other agencywide activities addressing cybersecurity workforce planning. However, all of the agencies GAO reviewed faced challenges determining the size of their cybersecurity workforce because of variations in how work is defined and the lack of an occupational series specific to cybersecurity. With respect to other workforce planning practices, all agencies had defined roles and responsibilities for their cybersecurity workforce, but these roles did not always align with guidelines issued by the federal Chief Information Officers Council and National Institute of Standards and Technology (NIST). Agencies reported challenges in filling highly technical positions, challenges due to the length and complexity of the federal hiring process, and discrepancies in compensation across agencies. Although most agencies used some form of incentives to support their cybersecurity workforce, none of the eight agencies had metrics to measure the effectiveness of these incentives. Finally, the robustness and availability of cybersecurity training and development programs varied significantly among the agencies. For example, the Departments of Commerce and Defense required cybersecurity personnel to obtain certifications and fulfill continuing education requirements. Other agencies used an informal or ad hoc approach to identifying required training.

The federal government has begun several governmentwide initiatives to enhance the federal cybersecurity workforce. The National Initiative for Cybersecurity Education, coordinated by NIST, includes activities to examine and more clearly define the federal cybersecurity workforce structure and roles and responsibilities, and to improve cybersecurity workforce training. However, the initiative lacks plans defining tasks and milestones to achieve its objectives, a clear list of agency activities that are part of the initiative, and a means to measure the progress of each activity. The Chief Information Officers Council, NIST, Office of Personnel Management, and the Department of Homeland Security (DHS) have also taken steps to define skills, competencies, roles, and responsibilities for the federal cybersecurity workforce. However, these efforts overlap and are potentially duplicative, although officials from these agencies reported beginning to take steps to coordinate activities. Furthermore, there is no plan to promote use of the outcomes of these efforts by individual agencies. The Office of Management and Budget and DHS have identified several agencies to be service centers for governmentwide cybersecurity training, but none of the service centers or DHS currently evaluates the training for duplicative content, effectiveness, or extent of use by federal agencies. The Scholarship for Service program, run by the National Science Foundation, is a small though useful source of new talent for the federal government, but the program lacks data on whether its participants remain in the government long-term.

_____ **United States Government Accountability Office**

Contents

Abbreviations

CIO	Chief Information Officer
Commerce	Department of Commerce
DHS	Department of Homeland Security
DOD	Department of Defense
DOT	Department of Transportation
FBI	Federal Bureau of Investigation
FedCTE	Federal Cybersecurity Training Event
FISMA	Federal Information Security Management Act
FedVTE	Federal Virtual Training Environment
FTE	full time equivalent
GS	General Schedule
HHS	Department of Health and Human Services
IT	information technology
Justice	Department of Justice
NASA	National Aeronautics and Space Administration
NICE	National Initiative for Cybersecurity Education
NIST	National Institute of Standards and Technology
NSA	National Security Agency
NSF	National Science Foundation
OMB	Office of Management and Budget
OPM	Office of Personnel Management
SFS	Scholarship for Service
SP	Special Publication
State	Department of State
Treasury	Department of the Treasury
VA	Department of Veterans Affairs

G A O
Accountability * Integrity * Reliability

United States Government Accountability Office
Washington, DC 20548

November 29, 2011

The Honorable Charles E. Schumer
Chairman
Subcommittee on Immigration, Refugees,
and Border Security
Committee on the Judiciary
United States Senate

Dear Mr. Chairman:

Federal electronic information and infrastructure are under attack from both domestic and foreign attackers who wish to penetrate and harm our networks. Threats to federal information technology (IT) infrastructure continue to grow in number and sophistication, posing a risk to the reliable functioning of our government. Securing federal networks is an evolving challenge for many reasons, including the anonymity of the Internet and because of the ever-changing nature of technology. In discussing his 2009 Cyberspace Policy Review,[1] President Obama declared the cyber threat to be "One of the most serious economic and national security challenges we face as a nation." Since 1997, we have identified the protection of federal information systems as a high-risk area for the government.[2] Essential to protecting our information and infrastructure is having a resilient, well-trained, and dedicated cybersecurity workforce.

Accordingly, as agreed with your office, the objectives of our review were to assess (1) the extent to which key federal agencies have implemented established workforce planning practices for cybersecurity personnel and (2) the status of and plans for governmentwide cybersecurity workforce initiatives. To address the first objective, we reviewed information related to workforce planning at the eight federal agencies and their components that have the highest budgets for IT: the Departments of Defense (DOD), Homeland Security (DHS), Health and Human Services (HHS), Treasury,

---

[1] President Barack Obama, "Cyberspace Policy Review: Assuring a Trusted and Resilient Information and Communications Infrastructure" (Washington, D.C.: May 29, 2009).

[2] See GAO, *High Risk Series: An Update*, GAO-11-278 (Washington, D.C.: February 2011).

Veterans Affairs (VA), Commerce, Transportation (DOT), and Justice. We used this information to evaluate each agency's efforts to identify critical cybersecurity skills and competencies needed, challenges in developing or obtaining the skills and competencies, and plans to address the challenges based on leading practices in workforce planning. To address our second objective, at agencies and organizations with specific governmentwide cybersecurity responsibilities, such as the National Institute of Standards and Technology (NIST), the Office of Personnel Management (OPM), the federal Chief Information Officers (CIO) Council, DHS, the National Science Foundation (NSF), and the Office of Management and Budget (OMB), we assessed plans and other efforts to coordinate cybersecurity workforce initiatives against leading practices in program management.

We conducted this performance audit at the agencies previously named in and around Washington, D.C., from December 2010 to November 2011, in accordance with generally accepted government auditing standards. Those standards require that we plan and perform the audit to obtain sufficient, appropriate evidence to provide a reasonable basis for our findings and conclusions based on our audit objectives. We believe that the evidence obtained provides a reasonable basis for our findings and conclusions based on our audit objectives. Further details on our objectives, scope, and methodology are contained in appendix I.

Background

Federal agencies have become increasingly dependent on electronic networks to carry out their operations. Virtually all federal operations are supported by automated systems and electronic data, and agencies would find it difficult, if not impossible, to carry out their missions, deliver services to the public, and account for their resources without these electronic information assets. The security of these systems is especially important to ensure the confidentiality, integrity, and availability of the information that resides on them. Conversely, ineffective information security can result in significant risk to a broad array of government operations and assets. Specifically,

- Resources, such as federal payments and collections, could be lost or stolen.

- Computer resources could be used for unauthorized purposes or to launch attacks on other computer systems.

- Sensitive information, such as taxpayer data, Social Security records, medical records, intellectual property, and proprietary business information, could be inappropriately disclosed, browsed, or copied for purposes of identity theft, espionage, or other types of crime.

- Critical operations, such as those supporting critical infrastructure, financial systems, national defense, and emergency services, could be exploited, disrupted, or destroyed.

Because of the importance of federal information systems to government operations, and because of continuing weaknesses in the information security controls over these systems, we have identified federal information security as a governmentwide high-risk area since 1997.[3]

Threats to federal information systems can be internal or external, accidental or targeted. They can range from individual hackers looking to do some mischief to terrorists or organized, state-sponsored groups looking to steal information or launch a cyber attack to cripple critical infrastructure. Recently, the Commander of the U.S. Cyber Command stated that "even the most astute malicious cyber actors—those who can break into almost any network that they really try to penetrate—are usually searching for targets of opportunity. They search for easy vulnerabilities in our systems' security and then exploit them."[4]

Cybersecurity professionals help to prevent or mitigate these vulnerabilities that could allow malicious individuals and groups access to federal IT systems. Specifically, the ability to secure federal systems is dependent on the knowledge, skills, and abilities of the federal and contractor workforce that uses, implements, secures, and maintains these systems. This includes federal and contractor employees who use the IT systems in the course of their work and the designers, developers, programmers, and administrators of the programs and systems.

---

[3]GAO-11-278.

[4]General Keith B. Alexander, in a statement before the House Committee on Armed Services, Subcommittee on Emerging Threats and Capabilities, Washington, D.C., March 16, 2011.

Several organizations have identified challenges facing the federal cybersecurity workforce. In July 2009, the Partnership for Public Service[5] reported challenges to maintaining the quality and quantity of the federal cybersecurity workforce, including the following:

- Federal cybersecurity workforce planning and decision making is decentralized across agencies.

- Agencies cannot readily identify the size of their cybersecurity workforce.

- Complicated rules and processes hamper recruiting and retention efforts.

In 2010, the Center for Strategic and International Studies reported[6] a shortage of qualified cybersecurity professionals in the United States, including those who can design secure systems, write secure computer code, and create the tools needed to prevent, detect, mitigate, and reconstitute information systems. According to the report, an organization's cybersecurity strategy should

- use hiring, acquisition, and training to raise the level of technical competence of those who build, operate, and protect government systems;

- establish a career path that rewards and retains those with the appropriate technical skills; and

- support development and adoption of rigorous technical certifications.

Within the federal government, others have identified cybersecurity-related workforce challenges at federal agencies. In September 2009, the Department of Commerce Inspector General reported that the department needed to devote more attention to the development and management of its cybersecurity personnel, and cited problems with training, performance

---

[5]Partnership for Public Service and Booz Allen Hamilton, *Cyber In-Security Strengthening the Federal Cybersecurity Workforce* (Washington, D.C.: July 22, 2009).

[6]Center for Strategic and International Studies, *A Human Capital Crisis in Cybersecurity— Technical Proficiency Matters* (Washington, D.C.: April 2010).

GAO-12-8 Cybersecurity Human Capital

management, and accountability of cybersecurity staff in the department.[7] In June 2010, the DHS Inspector General reported that difficulties filling vacant positions at the department's National Cyber Security Division were hampering its ability to achieve its mission.[8] In March 2011, the Commander of the U.S. Cyber Command testified that the military did not have enough highly skilled personnel to address the current and future cyber threats to our infrastructure.[9] Finally, in April 2011, the Inspector General at the Department of Justice reported that more than one-third of field agents interviewed for an audit reported that they lacked sufficient expertise to investigate the national security-related cyber intrusion cases that they had been assigned.[10]

Agencies Vary in Their Use of Workforce Planning Practices for Cybersecurity

Developing a strong workforce requires planning to acquire, develop, and retain it. Agency approaches to such planning can vary with the agency's particular needs and mission. Nevertheless, our own work and the work of other organizations, such as OPM,[11] suggest that there are leading practices that workforce planning should address, such as

- Developing workforce plans that link to the agency's strategic plan. Among other things, these plans should identify activities required to carry out the goals and objectives of the agency's strategic plan and include analysis of the current workforce to meet long-term and short-term goals and objectives.

---

[7]Commerce Office of Inspector General, *Commerce Should Take Steps to Strengthen Its IT Security Workforce*, CAR-19569-1 (Washington D.C.: September 2009).

[8]DHS Office of Inspector General, *U.S. Computer Emergency Readiness Team Makes Progress in Securing Cyberspace, but Challenges Remain*, OIG-10-94 (Washington D.C.: June 7, 2010).

[9]Alexander statement.

[10]Justice Office of the Inspector General, *The Federal Bureau of Investigation's Ability to Address the National Security Cyber Intrusion Threat*, Audit Report 11-22 (Washington D.C.: April 2011).

[11]GAO, *Human Capital: Key Principles for Effective Strategic Workforce Planning*, GAO-04-39 (Washington D.C.: Dec. 11, 2003); *A Model Of Strategic Human Capital Management*, GAO-02-373SP (Washington D.C.: Mar. 15, 2002); *Human Capital: A Self-Assessment Checklist for Agency Leaders*, GAO/OCG-00-14G (Washington D.C.: September 2000); OPM, *Human Capital Assessment and Accountability Framework—Systems, Standards, and Metrics* (http://www.opm.gov/hcaaf_resource_center/).

- Identifying the type and number of staff needed for an agency to achieve its mission and goals.

- Defining roles, responsibilities, skills, and competencies for key positions.

- Developing strategies to address recruiting needs and barriers to filling cybersecurity positions.

- Ensuring compensation incentives and flexibilities are effectively used to recruit and retain employees for key positions.

- Ensuring compensation systems are designed to help the agency compete for and retain the talent it needs to attain its goals.

- Establishing a training and development program that supports the competencies the agency needs to accomplish its mission.

Development and Implementation of Workforce Plans that Link to Agency Strategic Plans and Define Cybersecurity Workforce Needs Vary by Agency

Preparing a strategic workforce plan encourages agency managers and stakeholders to systematically consider what is to be done, when and how it will be done, what skills will be needed, and how to gauge progress and results. In addition, as part of its Human Capital Assessment and Accountability Framework, OPM requires agencies to maintain a current human capital plan and submit an annual human capital accountability report.[12] Agency approaches to such planning can vary with each agency's particular needs and mission. Nevertheless, existing strategic workforce planning tools and models and our own work suggest that there are key principles that such a process should address irrespective of the context in which the planning is done (see fig. 1).

---

[12]5 CFR § 250.203 (2011).

Figure 1: Strategic Workforce Planning Process

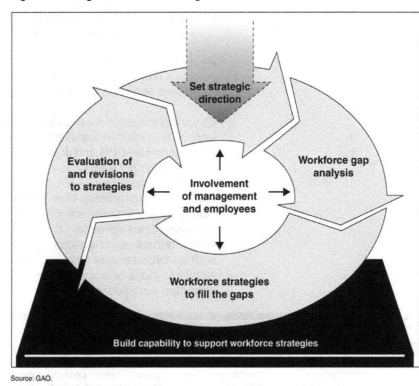

Source: GAO.

These key principles to address strategic workforce planning are to[13]

- involve top management, employees, and other stakeholders in developing, communicating, and implementing the strategic workforce plan;

- determine the critical skills and competencies that will be needed to achieve current and future programmatic results;

- develop strategies that are tailored to address gaps in number, deployment, and alignment of human capital approaches for enabling

[13]GAO-04-39.

and sustaining the contributions of all critical skills and competencies;

- build the capability needed to address administrative, educational, and other requirements important to support workforce strategies; and

- monitor and evaluate the agency's progress toward its human capital goals and the contribution that human capital results have made toward achieving programmatic goals.

Of the eight agencies we reviewed, two agencies—DOD and DOT—have workforce plans that specifically define cybersecurity workforce needs. Two agencies—DHS and Justice—have departmentwide workforce plans that, although not specific to cybersecurity, do address cybersecurity personnel. One agency—VA—has a guide on implementing competency models[14] that addresses elements of workforce planning, although it has neither a cybersecurity nor a departmentwide workforce plan. The remaining three agencies—Commerce, HHS, and Treasury—have neither departmental workforce plans nor workforce plans that specifically address cybersecurity workforce needs. Regarding the agencies with workforce plans or a competency guide, table 1 illustrates which key principles were addressed.

Table 1: Key Principles Addressed by Agency Workforce Plans

Agency	Involve top management, employees, and other stakeholders	Determine critical skills and competencies	Develop strategies that are tailored to address gaps in human capital approaches and critical skills and competencies	Build the capability needed to address requirements to support workforce strategies	Monitor and evaluate the agency's progress
DOD	yes	yes	partial	partial	yes
DHS	yes	yes	yes	yes	yes
Justice	yes	yes	yes	yes	yes
DOT	yes	yes	partial	partial	yes
VA	no	yes	partial	no	partial

Source: GAO analysis of agency workforce plans.

Note: Commerce, HHS, and Treasury did not provide either departmentwide or cybersecurity specific workforce plans. DOD and DOT had workforce plans that specifically defined cybersecurity workforce needs.

---

[14]A competency model identifies and describes a set of characteristics for a job description that are essential to effective performance of that position.

DOD has an information assurance workforce plan that describes the involvement of representatives of top management including the Chairman of the Joint Chiefs of Staff, the Under Secretary of Defense for Intelligence, the Defense Information Systems Agency, and the U.S. Strategic Command. The plan also incorporates critical skills, competencies, categories, and specialties of the information assurance workforce. However, the plan only partially describes strategies to address gaps in human capital approaches and critical skills and competencies. For example, the plan addresses gap analysis, education trends for the future IT workforce, identification and training of the current cybersecurity workforce, and recruitment and retention strategies. Additionally, the plan includes a timeline and goals to budget for, identify, train, and certify the DOD information assurance workforce over a 6-year period. However, the plan does not address performance management or recruiting flexibilities (e.g., alternative work schedules and special hiring authorities). In addition, the plan only partially describes building the capacity to support workforce strategies. Specifically, it states DOD will improve workforce processes, but does not discuss educating managers and employees on the use of recruiting flexibilities, having clear guidelines for using specific flexibilities, and holding managers and supervisors accountable for their effective use.

DHS has a departmentwide IT strategic human capital plan, although not a specific workforce plan for cybersecurity. The IT strategic human capital plan describes top management involvement and details workforce demographics and an IT occupational series that includes many of the department's cybersecurity positions. The plan also includes developing strategies to address workforce issues and states that DHS will develop IT competency models (including leadership competencies, project/program management, and others) that will identify behaviors, skills, and abilities needed to support DHS's mission requirements and provide a foundation for recruitment, career development, performance management, and employee recognition. The plan also discusses building the capacity to address requirements to support workforce strategies by improving workforce processes and developing metrics to assess human capital performance. In addition, the plan addresses the following objectives: IT talent acquisition and branding, IT employee development and retention, IT workforce performance, and IT workforce capacity.

Similarly, Justice has a departmentwide workforce plan, although not a specific workforce plan for cybersecurity. The departmentwide plan includes evidence of senior management coordination among multiple department components. In addition, the plan identifies critical skills and workforce information such as projected requirements and strategies for addressing gaps for many occupations including that of information technology specialist, which includes many of the department's cybersecurity positions. The plan also discusses developing strategies to address workforce issues such as how Justice will use various efforts to build the workforce, including identifying future IT workforce competency and skill requirements and developing recruitment and training activities. Further, the plan addresses building the capacity to address requirements such as how Justice will develop programs and improve processes to grow a workforce that can achieve the goals and meet the current and future challenges of the department's mission. In addition, the plan states that Justice will develop innovative programs, improve performance and accountability, and focus on performance metrics and measures.

DOT has a cybersecurity strategic plan that addresses workforce issues. Specifically, the plan discusses involvement of the Office of the CIO and other business owners. It identifies and defines roles specific to information security, such as the roles for chief information security officer, systems operations and maintenance professional, and network security specialist. However, the plan only partially outlines developing strategies to address gaps in human capital approaches and critical skills and competencies. For example, it states that DOT will develop the workforce, including upgrading the skill sets of its technical workforce and improving on the general skill sets of DOT employees and contractors. The plan also addresses gaps in workforce number and performance. However, the plan does not discuss hiring flexibilities and succession planning. In addition, the plan only partially addresses elements of building the capacity to support workforce strategies since the plan does not address educating managers and employees on the availability and use of recruiting flexibilities.

Finally, VA has developed a competency model guide that agency officials stated was used for workforce planning, although the agency did not have a specific workforce plan for cybersecurity or a departmentwide workforce plan. The guide includes skills and competencies needed at the agency. However, it does not address the involvement of top management in workforce planning. In addition, the guide only partially addresses developing strategies to address gaps in human capital approaches and critical skills and competencies. Specifically, the guide discusses needed data calls and budget forecasts and the importance of offering clear career paths, training, and professional development for critical IT positions. However, the guide does not address hiring flexibilities and succession planning. Furthermore, it does not address building the capacity to address requirements to support workforce strategies such as educating managers on the availability and use of flexibilities, streamlining and improving administrative processes, or building accountability into the system. In addition, the guide only partially addresses how the department will monitor and evaluate the agency's progress toward its human capital goals. Specifically, the guide discusses tracking employee progress in training and completion of tasks, but does not specifically mention monitoring and evaluation of agency implementation of its workforce plan or the outcomes of its human capital strategies. At the conclusion of our review, the department reported that it was initiating a departmentwide effort to identify and address its workforce planning needs.

Three agencies—Commerce, HHS, and Treasury—did not have a workforce plan for the department or one that specifically addressed cybersecurity workforce needs. These agencies reported different reasons for not having a cybersecurity workforce plan. For example, Commerce tracks cybersecurity workforce issues through reporting tools such as its balanced scorecard. The department stated it had defined necessary role-based training and skills for IT personnel with significant IT security roles and responsibilities. However, workforce planning is decentralized to its component organizations. The department provided evidence of steps it has been taking to oversee component cybersecurity workforce planning activities, such as recent compliance reviews, but acknowledged it did not have a detailed view of whether components were conducting workforce planning activities. At HHS, the Chief Information Security Officer stated that human capital requirements are determined by individual offices and are addressed during the department's budget development and justification process, and while the department has not formally defined the size of its cybersecurity workforce needs, it has documented plans for hiring, recruiting, and retaining personnel that map to recent OPM initiatives to streamline hiring. Finally, the Treasury Associate Chief Human Capital Officer indicated that workforce planning efforts are at the discretion of each of its component bureaus and stated that she believed the department's bureaus were performing the necessary workforce planning. At the conclusion of our audit, Treasury officials stated that the department had formed a workforce planning group to standardize processes to better conduct agencywide workforce planning.

Our prior work has shown that a workforce plan can help agencies define human capital goals and measure progress toward those goals. While the exact structure and level of centralization of such a plan may vary by agency, having some form of centralized oversight is crucial to effective management and accountability. In August 2011, OMB explicitly singled out information security as a primary responsibility for agency CIOs at all federal agencies.[15] Until all agencies establish workforce plans to address cybersecurity or ensure that their components are establishing such a plan, the ability of the agency's CIO to ensure cybersecurity staff are able to support the agency's information security goals may be limited.

Agencies Have Difficulty Identifying the Size of Their Cybersecurity Workforce

Successful human capital management and workforce planning are dependent on having and using valid and reliable data. These data can help an agency determine performance objectives, goals, the appropriate number of employees, and develop strategies to address gaps in the number, deployment, and alignment of employees.

However, the agencies we reviewed do not have consistent data on the size of their cybersecurity workforce. Table 2 presents cybersecurity workforce data for these agencies from four different sources:

- Data gathered by OMB as part of its reporting requirements under the Federal Information Security Management Act (FISMA).[16] In March 2011, OMB reported the total number of full-time equivalents (FTEs)[17] with major information security responsibilities at the eight agencies we reviewed—both federal employees and contractors—was about 75,000. Of these, approximately 49,000 were federal FTEs and approximately 25,000 were contractor FTEs.

- The number of employees with significant information security responsibilities reported by each agency in its FISMA report for fiscal year 2010.

---

[15]OMB, *M-11-29: Chief Information Officer Authorities* (Washington, D.C.: Aug. 8, 2011).

[16]Title III of the E-Government Act of 2002, Pub. L. No. 107-347, Dec. 17, 2002; OMB, *Fiscal Year 2010 Report to Congress on the Implementation of the Federal Information Security Management Act of 2002* (Washington, D.C.: Mar. 1, 2011).

[17]An FTE is the number of total hours worked divided by the maximum number of compensable hours in a work year. For example, if the work year is defined as 2,080 hours, then one worker occupying a paid full time job all year would consume one FTE. Two persons working for 1,040 hours each would consume one FTE between the two of them.

- Information gathered by OPM in 2010 as part of an informal data collection on the federal cybersecurity workforce. Six of the eight agencies we reviewed responded to OPM's data call, and in aggregate, they reported a total of about 35,000 workers engaged in cybersecurity work. However, it is not clear whether that number included the intelligence workforce and contractors.

- The results of our request to agencies to identify their number of cybersecurity employees.

Table 2: Comparison of Reported Number of Cybersecurity Workers from Multiple Sources

Agency	FTEs per OMB's Fiscal Year 2010 FISMA report	Personnel reported in 2010 agency FISMA report of personnel with significant information security responsibilities	Personnel per OPM 2010 data gathering	Personnel per GAO 2011 data call
Commerce	1,161	1,258	not reported	373
DOD	66,000	87,846	18,955	88,159
HHS	965	6,244	16	not reported
DHS	1,453	3,350	12,500	1,361
Justice	2,887	2,989	2,632	283
DOT	524	848	not reported	not reported
Treasury	1,175	7,833	734	904
VA	836	9,887	400	not reported

Source: GAO analysis of OMB and agency reports and agency-provided data.

Note: The numbers in the table are estimations, and do not include intelligence personnel for several agencies, including DOD and Justice.

The data provided vary widely based on specific data call requirements. For example, DOD reported about 87,000 FTEs with significant security responsibilities for its FISMA report, but just under 19,000 personnel in cybersecurity to OPM. VA was identified as having about 800 FTEs in OMB's FISMA report, but reported almost 9,900 personnel with significant security responsibilities in its agency FISMA report.

The difficulty in identifying the size of the cybersecurity workforce is partly due to the challenge of defining a cybersecurity worker. FISMA-related guidance asks federal agencies to track the number of personnel who have significant information security responsibilities and have received role-based security training each year. It is possible for an employee to perform a significant security responsibility, such as authorizing operation of a system, without that being the majority of his or her work. In addition, many employees may perform cybersecurity responsibilities as an additional duty and not as their primary job responsibility. During our review, we were asked by agencies to provide a more specific definition for cybersecurity staff, so we asked agencies to identify the number of employees who spend a majority of their time performing cybersecurity responsibilities.

Furthermore, there is no specific federal occupational series that identifies federal cybersecurity positions. A series is used to identify a specific occupation and generally includes all jobs in that particular kind of work at all grade levels. Many agencies use the occupational series developed by OPM. However, OPM's 2010 cybersecurity data collection showed that federal agencies used multiple series for their cybersecurity workforce. (See table 3.) None of these series identifies cybersecurity as the only job responsibility. In many cases, employees with cybersecurity responsibilities also have other responsibilities, and some employees classified under a particular series may not have any cybersecurity responsibilities.

Table 3: Occupational Series Commonly Used for Cybersecurity Workforce

Occupational series	Series group name
0080	Security administration series
0132	Intelligence series
0301	Miscellaneous administration and program series
0340	Program management series
0391	Telecommunications series
0801	General engineering series
0854	Computer engineering series
0855	Electronic engineering series
1101	General business and industry series
1301	General physical science series
1550	Computer science series
1801	General inspection, investigation, enforcement, and compliance series
1805	Investigative analysis series
1810	General investigation series
1811	Criminal investigation series
2010	Inventory management series
2210	Information technology management series

Source: GAO summary, based on OPM's responses and General Schedule.

The 2210 series, information technology management, has a parenthetical title, a form of subclassification, which can be used to identify information security positions. Six of the eight agencies we reviewed primarily used this series for their cybersecurity workforce. However, the parenthetical title is not used consistently at the federal agencies we reviewed.

Even within an agency there is inconsistency in defining cybersecurity positions. For example, we previously reported[18] that DOD lacked a common definition for cybersecurity personnel among the different services, which created challenges in determining adequate types and numbers of cybersecurity personnel.

While several agency officials stated that a single occupational series for cybersecurity would make collecting information on their cybersecurity workforce easier, both they and OPM identified additional problems this could create in not accurately reflecting the noncybersecurity work that a particular employee may perform, and in limiting an employee's career mobility. As a result, although OPM officials stated that currently there is no way other than creating an occupational series to allow easy identification of cybersecurity employees governmentwide, OPM is not planning to create such a job series. They stated that determining a way to track federal cybersecurity personnel is to be part of future efforts to reform federal personnel systems, but did not yet have specific milestones or tasks for doing so.

The difficulties in identifying the cybersecurity workforce mean that most of the agencies we reviewed rely on manual processes to gather information on their workforce. Only two of the eight agencies we reviewed—Commerce and Treasury—were able to use an automated agencywide process to collect FISMA-related training information. However, a manager within the Office of the CIO at Commerce stated that the information collected by Commerce's system may not be entirely comprehensive, and Treasury officials reported that there were still certain manual data-gathering steps that fed into the automated system.

The large variation in the numbers reported to OMB, OPM, and us demonstrates the difficulties that agencies face in accurately tracking their cybersecurity workforce. It also illustrates the difficulties in relying on

---

[18]GAO, *Defense Department Cyber Efforts: DOD Faces Challenges in Its Cyber Activities*, GAO-11-75 (Washington D.C.: July 25, 2011).

these numbers for workforce planning activities. However, developing a means to track the cybersecurity workforce will require a governmentwide effort to improve personnel systems. Until these improvements are made, agencies will continue to have difficulty gathering accurate data on the existing size of their cybersecurity workforce and making data-driven decisions for cybersecurity workforce planning.

Agencies Have Taken Steps to Define Cybersecurity Roles and Responsibilities and Related Skills and Competencies, but Lack Clear Guidance

We have previously reported that agencies should develop and adopt clearly defined roles and responsibilities and related skills and competencies to help ensure that personnel have the appropriate workload, skills, and training to perform their jobs effectively. In addition, we have stated that federal agencies that ensure they have high-performing employees with the appropriate skills and competencies are better able to meet their mission and goals.[19]

Several federal organizations have provided guidelines and tools for agencies to define cybersecurity roles and responsibilities. Specifically,

- The CIO Council has developed the following 11 cybersecurity roles, most recently updated in October 2010, that agencies can use as guidelines in developing detailed position descriptions and training.[20]

  - chief information officer
  - chief information security officer
  - digital forensics and incident response analyst
  - information security assessor
  - information security risk analyst
  - information systems security officer
  - information security systems and software development specialist
  - network security specialist
  - security architect
  - systems operations and maintenance professional
  - vulnerability analyst.

---

[19]GAO-04-39 and GAO, *Comptroller's Forum, High Performing Organizations: Metrics, Means, and Mechanisms for Achieving High Performance in the 21st Century Public Management Environment*, GAO-04-343SP (Washington, D.C.: Feb. 13, 2004).

[20]The CIO Council is chaired by the Deputy Director for Management of OMB and has members from 28 federal agencies.

- NIST has described roles and responsibilities in Special Publication 800-37. This publication describes the roles and responsibilities of the key participants involved in an organization's risk management process including, among others, the chief information officer, information owner, senior information security officer, information system owner, information system security officer, and information security architect.[21] Additional NIST publications also define other cybersecurity roles and responsibilities.

- OPM developed a competency model for cybersecurity, released in February 2011, that lists key competencies for the cybersecurity workforce. OPM, in collaboration with an interagency working group, has also developed three broad categories for cybersecurity work: IT infrastructure, operations, maintenance, and information assurance; domestic law enforcement and counterintelligence; and specialized, and largely classified, cybersecurity operations focused on collection, exploitation, and response.

Federal agencies we reviewed had generally taken steps to fully or partially define cybersecurity roles and responsibilities and related skills and competencies based in part on these guidelines. For example,

- Commerce had defined operational roles, responsibilities, skills, and competencies for multiple cybersecurity roles based on Special Publication 800-37. The agency also defined skills and competencies through its training policy. For example, for the information system owner role, Commerce identified training and certifications that support the defined role based on competencies that the department identified.

- DOD had performed extensive work to outline roles, responsibilities, skills, and competencies in its cybersecurity workforce. DOD Directive 8570.01-M[22] defines the roles, responsibilities, competencies, and skills that DOD expects its cybersecurity workforce to possess. For example, the role of information assurance management level 1 is

---

[21]Department of Commerce, National Institute of Standards and Technology, Special Publication 800-37 Revision 1, *Guide for Applying the Risk Management Framework to Federal Information Systems* (Gaithersburg, Md.: 2010).

[22]Department of Defense, DOD 8570.01-M, "Information Assurance Workforce Improvement Program" (Dec. 19, 2005).

defined as having responsibility for the implementation and operation of a DOD information system. Additionally, the directive outlines skills such as user validation and competencies such as information assurance that are critical to the job.

- HHS has developed definitions of cybersecurity roles and responsibilities and has developed partial definitions of skills and competencies at the agency level for these positions. The HHS Information Systems Security and Privacy policy defines 31 roles and their corresponding responsibilities for the agency's cybersecurity program based, in part, on NIST guidelines. According to agency officials, HHS uses shared position descriptions to document certain skills and competencies through the job analysis process but has not undertaken efforts to fully define skills and competencies for cybersecurity positions.

- DHS has issued guidance that defines roles, responsibilities, skills, and competencies for its cybersecurity workforce based on both CIO Council and NIST guidelines. However, according to agency officials, use of the guidance is not consistent across all components of the agency.

- Justice has only partially defined roles and responsibilities and skills and competencies. Specifically, while selected individual components have developed detailed definitions for roles, responsibilities, skills, and competencies, the agency has not developed an overarching definition for the entire agency. According to the agency, this is due, in part, to the specialized nature of the work performed by Justice components.

- DOT has defined roles and responsibilities and skills and competencies for cybersecurity staff based in part on NIST guidelines in its cybersecurity strategic plan; however, the department stated it does not have time frames for implementing its strategic plan because of limited funding.

- Treasury has partially defined roles, responsibilities, skills, and competencies for the agency. Treasury has departmentwide policy defining roles and responsibilities for the cybersecurity workforce, but officials reported that because of the department's decentralized nature, they do not manage how roles and responsibilities are defined at the bureau level. Furthermore, Treasury officials stated that they only define skills and competencies in specific position descriptions, although this is, to some extent, based on OPM's competency model.

- VA has partially defined roles, responsibilities, skills, and competencies for the agency based on CIO Council and OPM guidelines. For the information security officer role, VA has defined a model that includes an extensive training program that addresses roles and responsibilities and needed skills and competencies. However, VA has not yet defined roles, responsibilities, skills, and competencies for the cybersecurity workforce except for the information security officer role. According to VA officials, the agency is planning on extending this model to other positions in the cybersecurity workforce but does not yet have estimated completion dates.

The approaches taken by each agency to define cybersecurity roles, responsibilities, skills, and competencies vary considerably. Some of these differences can be attributed to differences in mission, goals, and organization. For example, officials within components of Justice—the Federal Bureau of Investigation (FBI) and Computer Crime and Intellectual Property Section—stated that certain aspects of their work did not fit into governmentwide cybersecurity definitions. Treasury officials also stated that because of the decentralized structure of their department, it would be difficult to centralize definitions of roles and responsibilities.

However, many of the differences can be attributed to the multiple sources of governmentwide guidance and their lack of alignment. The agencies we reviewed reported drawing on, to varying extent, the CIO Council definitions, NIST publications, and the OPM competency model. However, these three models all take different approaches to defining the cybersecurity workforce. For example, the matrices supporting the CIO Council's effort use roles, performance level, competencies, skills, suggested credentials, and suggested training. NIST Special Publication 800-37 describes roles and responsibilities for cybersecurity based on FISMA-related responsibilities. OPM's competency model addresses cybersecurity professionals in terms of series, grade, and competencies. There are enough differences in these sources of guidance to cause confusion for agencies. For example, the CIO Council matrices define a chief information security officer role, which, according to the CIO Council project lead, maps to the NIST senior information security officer role. However, the NIST framework also defines other roles, such as information owner and authorizing official, that do not map to roles defined by the CIO Council. While both organizations define an information security assessor role, the CIO Council defines this role as being autonomous from the organization, while NIST states that the level of independence of the assessor varies based on the specific conditions of the role. Until these multiple governmentwide efforts are more clearly aligned, agencies may have difficulty consistently defining these areas for themselves and avoiding duplication of effort.

Agencies Report Challenges in Filling Cybersecurity Positions

A high-performance organization needs a workforce with talent, multidisciplinary knowledge, and up-to-date skills in order to achieve its mission.[23] To recruit such a workforce for cybersecurity, agencies should develop recruiting and hiring efforts that are tailored to address gaps in the number, skills, and competencies of their cybersecurity workforce. They should establish an active recruiting program with involvement from senior leaders and line managers and make use of strategies such as outreach to colleges and universities and internships.[24] In addition, administrative processes needed to hire a candidate should be streamlined to expedite hiring. An effective hiring process meets the needs of agencies and managers by filling positions with quality employees through the use of a timely, efficient, and transparent process.

Agencies' Ability to Fill Cybersecurity Positions Mixed

The agencies we reviewed varied in their ability to fill cybersecurity positions. (See table 4.) Specifically, officials at four of the eight agencies we reviewed stated that they were generally able to recruit and hire to fill needed cybersecurity positions. Officials at several agencies reported challenges in filling more technical positions, and officials at two agencies reported currently being under a hiring freeze.

---

[23]GAO, *Human Capital: Opportunities to Improve Executive Agencies' Hiring Processes*, GAO-03-450 (Washington, D.C.: May 30, 2003).

[24]GAO/OCG-00-14G.

Table 4: Summary of Agency Reported Status of Efforts to Fill Cybersecurity Positions

Agency	Reported status
Commerce	Generally is able to find sufficient applicants to fill positions but sometimes has difficulty finding candidates with a combination of federal experience, detailed IT security knowledge, and professional certifications.
DOD	Reported difficulties with recruiting qualified cybersecurity staff. Identified barriers include processing time for security clearances, difficulty finding qualified candidates, and the hiring process. Additionally, the National Security Agency (NSA) has expressed concern that the future pipeline of talent may not be able to meet the agency's needs.
HHS	Generally able to fill open positions, but reports difficulty meeting current cybersecurity responsibilities with the current level of staffing. The department's Chief Information Security Officer cited continuing findings in the HHS Inspector General's evaluations and audits of the agency's implementation of FISMA as evidence of a lack of sufficient head count.
DHS	Reported being able to find qualified cybersecurity staff to fill positions generally, but a component—the National Cyber Security Division—has had trouble finding personnel for certain specialized areas, such as watch officers.
Justice	Officials from both Justice's Computer Crime and Intellectual Property Section and its CIO organization stated that a current hiring freeze limits their ability to determine if recruiting is a challenge. Officials from both the CIO organization and FBI stated that entry-level cybersecurity positions have generally been easier to fill than positions requiring more advanced technical knowledge.
DOT	The department stated that a lack of funding has prevented DOT from hiring personnel to fill cybersecurity positions recently.
Treasury	Treasury stated that there can be difficulty filling more technical cybersecurity positions, such as those dealing with penetration testing and forensic analysis, but there is not a consensus across the organization that finding qualified staff is a problem.
VA	VA officials stated that they are able to find qualified staff but have difficulty retaining them once they are trained, as they leave for higher-paying federal or contractor positions.

Source: GAO summary of agency written responses and interviews.

In contrast to the other agencies we reviewed, only DOD provided specific numerical evidence of a shortage of cybersecurity personnel. DOD reported that for 2010, the department had more than 97,000 information assurance positions, but about 9,000 of these positions were unfilled. DOD's Cyber Command projected that as of September 2011, it would have more than 80 percent of available cyber positions filled. According to the department, its current vacancy level is due, in part, to Cyber Command being a relatively new organization, having been created in May 2010.

Officials at several agencies identified concerns with the availability of candidates for certain highly technical positions, such as network security engineers, malware analysts, and computer forensics experts. Specifically, Treasury and HHS officials stated that while they generally do not have problems filling cybersecurity positions, highly technical positions can be difficult to fill. Treasury officials stated that they use contractors to fill in the gaps for the hard-to-fill cybersecurity positions. Officials also identified challenges due to competition with both the private sector and other federal agencies that are able to offer more compensation for similar positions. In addition, officials at Commerce and DHS stated that they have not experienced difficulty in finding qualified cybersecurity staff for most positions, but have at times had trouble finding personnel who have the specialized skills they require.

Agencies Report Challenges with Administrative Processes, Including Hiring and Obtaining Security Clearances

Officials at the agencies we reviewed identified challenges with administrative processes for recruiting and hiring cybersecurity staff, including the length and complexity of the federal hiring process and delays in obtaining security clearances.

Specifically, officials at six of the eight agencies we reviewed identified the hiring process as an obstacle to hiring cybersecurity personnel. We have previously reported[25] and the administration has acknowledged[26] that the complexity and inefficiency of the federal hiring process has deterred many highly-qualified individuals from seeking and obtaining jobs. In order to recruit highly-qualified individuals such as those in security, some agencies stated they have used several different hiring authorities to help them recruit cybersecurity personnel; however, there was little documented evidence that suggested one particular hiring authority was more advantageous than another.[27] For example, some agencies use the direct hire authority or the excepted hire authority to recruit cybersecurity personnel, but they did not provide data on whether the different hiring authorities allowed them to hire more or better qualified cybersecurity professionals, or whether the hiring authority allowed them to bring the candidates aboard more quickly.

In May 2010, President Obama instructed federal executive agencies to streamline and improve the federal hiring process.[28] These changes

---

[25]GAO-03-450.

[26]The White House, Office of the Press Secretary, "Presidential Memorandum–Improving the Federal Recruitment and Hiring Process," Washington, D.C., May 11, 2010.

[27]Federal employees can be hired under several different hiring authorities, including competitive service (the standard hiring authority), excepted service, and direct hire authority. Each authority has different rules and regulations governing the selection of candidates, with the rules for excepted service and direct hire intended to make it easier or faster for agencies to hire personnel under certain circumstances.

[28]Presidential Memorandum–"Improving the Federal Recruitment and Hiring Process," May 11, 2010.

included reducing the time it takes to hire new employees to less than 80 days, eliminating essay-style questions from initial job applications in favor of résumés and cover letters, adopting a category rating system[29] to provide managers with a larger applicant pool from which to select candidates, and requiring hiring managers and supervisors to be more involved in the hiring process. All of these changes were to have been implemented by November 2010. Agencies were to report on their progress in implementing the hiring reforms to OPM.

All eight of the agencies we reviewed reported having begun implementing the reforms, with almost all agencies reporting continuing efforts to improve the hiring process. DOD officials cautioned that it would take time for the full effect of the reforms to spread across the department. And some agencies, such as Justice, noted that because of a hiring freeze, they had not hired new cybersecurity staff, making the effectiveness of the reforms difficult to judge. Table 5 summarizes agency adoption of the hiring reforms.

---

[29]Category rating allows hiring managers to select from among all candidates who are grouped in the highest-quality category for rating applications. The "rule of three," which was often used previously, limits hiring managers to selecting potential hires from only among the three highest-rated candidates.

Table 5: Agency-Reported Implementation of the President's May 2010 Hiring Reforms

Agency	Status of reform implementation
Commerce	Commerce's average time-to-hire in the third quarter of fiscal year 2011 was 75 days. Commerce officials reported the department had eliminated application essay questions in favor of résumés and implemented category rating for all of its hiring. Commerce did not provide data on improving manager involvement in the hiring process.
DOD	DOD's average time-to-hire in the third quarter of fiscal year 2011 was 70 days. DOD officials reported that work is ongoing to improve manager satisfaction with the quality of candidates and applicant satisfaction.
HHS	HHS's average time-to-hire in the third quarter of fiscal year 2011 was 52 business days. It has also implemented category rating departmentwide, and eliminated application essay questions in favor of résumés. HHS did not report on manager involvement in the hiring process because of low survey response rates.
DHS	DHS has eliminated application essay questions in favor of résumés, started to implement category ratings for all of its hiring, and reported training its managers and supervisors to be more involved in the hiring process, but did not report its average time-to-hire.
Justice	Justice officials reported that the department had implemented the hiring reforms, and indicated it has policies for the use of category rating, but provided no data on its elimination of application essay questions in favor of résumés, manager involvement in the hiring process, or its average time-to-hire.
DOT	DOT's average time-to-hire in the second quarter of fiscal year 2011 was 123 days. DOT officials reported implementing a category rating system, eliminating application essay questions in favor of résumés, and taking steps to increase manager involvement in the hiring process.
Treasury	Treasury's average time-to-hire in the second quarter of fiscal year 2011 was 129 days. Treasury officials reported having implemented category rating departmentwide, and eliminated application essay questions in favor of résumés.
VA	VA reported an average time-to-hire of 95 days as of August 2011. The department also reported that it has eliminated application essay questions in favor of résumés, implemented category rating, and taken steps to increase managers' involvement in the hiring process.

Source: GAO summary of agency documentation.

Obtaining a security clearance for new employees was also identified by several officials as a challenge. For example, DOD's Cyber Command reported that it can take about a year to start a new employee because of both the lengthy hiring process and the time required to obtain a security clearance. We have previously reported on the challenges in timely adjudication of security clearance applications for federal employees and contractors, identifying delays in DOD's security clearance process as a high-risk area since 2005.[30] FBI reported continuing challenges with both obtaining initial clearances and processing clearances for cleared employees at other federal agencies that transfer to FBI. We recently

---

[30]GAO, *High-Risk Series: An Update,* GAO-05-207 (Washington, D.C.: January 2005), and *DOD Personnel Clearances: Comprehensive Timeliness Reporting, Complete Clearance Documentation, and Quality Measures Are Needed to Further Improve the Clearance Process,* GAO-09-400 (Washington, D.C.: May 19, 2009).

reported that agencies had made substantial progress in reducing the time to obtain security clearances, and removed DOD's clearance process from our high-risk list in February 2011, but also reported that continuing work was needed in this area.[31]

Agency Use of Incentives to Recruit and Retain Cybersecurity Personnel Varies; Few Metrics Exist to Measure Their Effectiveness

Federal agencies have the authority to offer a variety of incentives to attract and retain personnel with the critical skills needed to accomplish their missions. These incentives can include recruitment, relocation, and retention incentive payments; student loan repayments; annual leave enhancements; scholarships; and student employment programs. Each agency has the flexibility to determine which specific incentives of those authorized it chooses to offer.[32] If an agency offers recruitment, relocation, or retention incentives, it is required by regulation to track their implementation.[33] Furthermore, we have previously reported on the importance of establishing the necessary data and indicators to track an incentive program's effectiveness, as well as establishing a baseline to measure the changes over time and assess the program in the future.[34]

Several agencies and components of the agencies that we reviewed reported incentive programs that they have used for hiring and retaining cybersecurity personnel. (See table 6.)

[31]GAO, *Personnel Security Clearances: Progress Has Been Made to Improve Timeliness, but Continued Oversight Is Needed to Sustain Momentum*, GAO-11-65 (Washington, D.C.: Nov. 19. 2010), and GAO-11-278.

[32]According to OPM, an agency may also use additional incentives, such as special pay rates and recruitment, retention, and relocation incentives in excess of predefined limits by seeking approval from OPM.

[33]5 CFR § 575.112, 5 CFR § 575.212, 5 CFR § 575.312.

[34]GAO, *Human Capital: Continued Opportunities Exist for FDA and OPM to Improve Oversight of Recruitment, Relocation, and Retention Incentives*, GAO-10-226 (Washington, D.C.: Jan. 22, 2010).

Table 6: Reported Use of Incentives for Cybersecurity Workforce Recruiting and Retention at Selected Federal Agencies

Incentive	Commerce	DOD	HHS	DHS	Justice	DOT[a]	Treasury[b]	VA
Recruitment incentives	X	X		X	X			
Relocation incentives		X		X	X			
Retention incentives	X	X			X			
Superior qualifications and special needs pay-setting authority[c]	X	X		X	X			
Scholarships[d]		X						
Student employment programs	X	X			X			
Student loan repayments	X	X			X			
Annual leave enhancements		X		X	X			

Source: GAO analysis of agency documentation.

[a] DOT indicated it does not use scholarships or student loan repayments for cybersecurity recruiting at a department level, but the Federal Aviation Administration, a component of DOT, does make use of them.

[b] Treasury indicated that it does not make use of retention incentives or superior qualifications and special needs pay setting authority for cybersecurity employees, but the Internal Revenue Service, a component of Treasury, does make use of them.

[c] The superior qualifications and special needs pay setting authority allows an agency to set the rate of basic pay of an individual newly appointed to a General Schedule position at a rate above the minimum rate of the appropriate General Schedule grade based on the employee's superior qualifications or a special need of the agency.

[d] Refers to scholarships that are offered and funded by the agency we reviewed and does not count scholarships that are funded by an outside source such as the Scholarship for Service program.

Among the agencies we reviewed, DOD offered the broadest range of incentives to recruit and retain cybersecurity professionals. For example, DOD had scholarship programs, student employment programs, and recruitment incentives that can be offered to cybersecurity professionals or individuals who are studying to become cybersecurity professionals. In addition, DOD is seeking new authorities and incentives in order to improve its ability to recruit cybersecurity talent. These authorities range from expanded scholarships to retention incentives that are dependent on cybersecurity certifications.

At other agencies, incentives were less specifically focused on the cybersecurity workforce. Instead, agencies made targeted use of existing authorities and incentives in order to attract the individuals with the skills that they needed. For example,

- DHS reported using incentives including recruitment and relocation incentives, superior qualifications and special needs pay setting authority, and annual leave enhancements, and plans to offer student loan repayments when negotiating with potential employees.

- Justice reported using incentives including recruiting, relocation, and retention incentives; superior qualifications and special needs pay setting authority; student employment programs; student loan repayments; and annual leave enhancements. Justice officials reported that use of these incentives is guided by departmental policy.

- Treasury components are permitted to use incentives, but have generally not found it necessary to employ them or do not have sufficient funds to use them. The Internal Revenue Service uses retention incentives and superior qualifications and special needs pay setting authority in lieu of other recruitment incentives.

Several agencies reported not using incentives, or using them sparingly. As noted, Treasury reported it had generally not found incentives to be necessary to recruit or retain cybersecurity workers. HHS reported that, given the state of the economy, it found it had large applicant pools to select from when hiring cybersecurity workers, making it unnecessary to use incentives. In addition, officials from FBI and the National Security Agency (NSA) told us that the unique missions of the organizations serve as a strong incentive for potential employees and compensate for lower salaries. Officials at VA said they were developing an incentive program.

Officials at several of the agencies we reviewed stated that they do not evaluate or have difficulty evaluating whether incentives effectively support hiring and retaining highly-skilled personnel in hard-to-fill positions. For example, DOD stated that the fact that its civilian incentive programs are neither centrally managed nor limited to selected occupational specialties makes it difficult to determine how effective the incentives are in retaining cybersecurity professionals. A Treasury official reported that because of the decentralized nature of the department and the difficulties in categorizing cybersecurity personnel, the department does not know the full extent of its use of incentives for cybersecurity recruiting and retention. Justice officials stated that, since incentive recipients must sign service agreements requiring them to work for the department for a set period of time, there is no need to perform any other kind of tracking.

Governmentwide evaluation of the effectiveness of incentives is also limited. During calendar years 2005 through 2009, Congress required OPM to produce annual governmentwide reports on the use of recruitment, relocation, and retention incentives at the series and grade levels. However, as previously discussed, cybersecurity responsibilities do not necessarily correspond to a specific job series. In August 2011, OPM reported that in calendar year 2009, federal agencies paid approximately $14.2 million in recruitment, relocation, and retention incentives to 1,269 IT workers in the 2210 occupation series, under which many, but not all, cybersecurity employees are classified.[35] In this report, OPM stated these incentives are important tools to help agencies attract and retain employees. However, OPM also stated its report is not intended to provide detailed information on the content or administration of agency incentive plans and policies, and that it does not verify the quality or accuracy of the agency-submitted data upon which it bases its report. Since the congressional mandate for this report has expired, OPM has issued proposed regulations that would continue the data gathering and reporting as an ongoing activity. In commenting on a draft of this report, OPM provided additional information on steps it was taking to improve oversight of incentives, including requesting updated baseline data on the use of incentives from agencies for calendar years 2010 and 2011, and setting limits on spending for incentives in calendar years 2011 and 2012.

We previously found that agencies had opportunities to improve oversight of their use of incentives,[36] and OPM has found that agencies' oversight of their incentives was not sufficient.[37] In February 2010, OPM outlined a plan to improve the oversight of the use of recruitment, relocation, and retention incentives governmentwide. As part of this plan, OPM has stated it would develop additional guidance and tools to assist agencies in the administration and oversight of their incentive programs, but has not yet done so. While the proposed regulations OPM issued would expand the scope of existing regulations by requiring agencies to review all retention incentives and recruitment incentives targeted at groups of employees at least annually to determine whether they should be revised

---

[35]OPM, *Recruitment, Relocation and Retention Incentives Calendar Year 2009 Report to the Congress* (Washington, D.C.: August 2011).

[36]GAO-10-226.

[37]OPM, *Plan to Improve the Administration and Oversight of Recruitment, Relocation and Retention Incentives* (Washington, D.C.: Feb. 3, 2010).

or discontinued, these regulations have not been finalized.[38] Without finalized guidance from OPM, agencies will likely continue to face challenges in determining the effectiveness of their incentives in recruiting and retaining cybersecurity employees.

Differences in Compensation Systems Create Perception of Disparity in Agencies' Ability to Recruit and Retain Cybersecurity Professionals

A compensation system is a tool for attracting, motivating, retaining, and rewarding the people an agency needs to accomplish its mission and goals. Organizations examine their compensation systems to identify relevant constraints and flexibilities and make changes to support their human capital needs. Generally, the agencies we reviewed are subject to the General Schedule (GS) system of position classifications and grades to define positions and set salaries. In certain cases where agencies have had difficulty recruiting and retaining IT employees, OPM has authorized agencies to pay salaries higher than those under the regular GS system. We, the National Commission on the Public Service, and OPM have all called for the reform or replacement of the GS system and related performance management systems, citing factors including its inflexibility and its reliance on time in position rather than performance as a means of motivating and rewarding employees.[39]

Officials at two of the eight agencies we reviewed, as well as at OPM, said they believed the pay and flexibilities offered to applicants at agencies or agency components that do not use the GS system make those agencies more attractive to applicants, as compared with agencies that use the GS system. Officials at DHS and OPM identified NSA, and Treasury officials identified some of its own bureaus, such as the Office of the Comptroller of the Currency, as non-GS agencies that were more competitive when recruiting cybersecurity applicants, as they could offer higher salaries to cybersecurity employees than allowed under the GS

---

[38]In commenting on a draft of this report, OPM stated that when the regulations are finalized they are l kely to contain criteria for these annual reviews similar to criteria in existing OPM regulations.

[39]GAO-03-450; National Commission on the Public Service, *Urgent Business for America—Revitalizing The Federal Government for The 21st Century*, (Washington, D.C.: Jan. 2003); and OPM, *A Fresh Start for Federal Pay: The Case for Modernization* (Washington, D.C.: April 2002). In addition, in commenting on a draft of this report, OPM stated that the Director of OPM has taken more recent steps toward improved performance management through participation in governmentwide working groups.

system. However, as previously noted, DHS and Treasury stated that they are generally able to fill their cybersecurity positions.

For example, a flexibility in the compensation system NSA uses gives it a greater ability to pay employees more as they gain additional experience or responsibilities. The flexibility, called "rank-in-person," allows the agency to promote and pay an employee more as the employee gains additional experience or responsibilities without the employee needing to apply for a new position or requiring that a vacant position be available, as would be required under the GS system. In contrast, the GS system uses a "promotion-in-position" system, under which positions are classified at one or more grades (for example, GS-7, GS-9, GS-11, and GS-13). When an employee reaches the maximum salary permitted by the highest grade at which the position is classified, he or she must apply for a job classified at a higher grade to earn more. Furthermore, according to OPM, the salary at the highest step of a grade is only about 30 percent higher than the initial step, while alternative pay systems generally have considerably wider pay ranges. NSA officials stated that while they do not use the GS system's "promotion-in-position" system, NSA's hiring and personnel practices are more similar to those of the rest of the federal government than they are different. Table 7 summarizes some of the compensation flexibilities at non-GS-system components of agencies that we reviewed.

Table 7: Selected Compensation Flexibilities at Certain Non-GS-System Federal Agencies

Flexibility	Description
Pay banding	Salary ranges are set in 6-8 broad ranges (bands) rather than the 15 grades of the GS system.
Higher salaries	Agencies can offer higher salaries than at agencies that use the GS system.
Rank-in-person	Employee grade and pay levels are set based on the combination of qualifications and assignments, in addition to the responsibilities and duties of the position occupied.

Source: GAO analysis of agency data.

These differences in compensation systems among the agencies we reviewed have created the perception that agencies using non-GS compensation systems may have greater success in recruiting and retaining cybersecurity personnel. We have recently begun a review to examine previous recommendations to reform the federal pay systems. Identifying and implementing improvements to the GS pay and position classification systems may improve the government's ability to recruit and retain employees, including cybersecurity employees.

Training and Development Opportunities for Cybersecurity Workers Vary Widely among Agencies

Strategic human capital management centers on viewing people as assets whose value to an organization can be enhanced through investment in training and development activities to help employees build the competencies needed to achieve an agency's goals. We and OPM[40] have identified training programs and the earning of professional certifications as activities that support an employee's development of needed skills and competencies. As set forth in our guide, to ensure that agencies are making appropriate investments in training and development, agencies should also make fact-based determinations of the impact of their training and development programs.

Table 8 summarizes agency use of cybersecurity training programs and certification requirements.

Table 8: Agency Cybersecurity Training and Development Programs and Practices

Agency	Training program	Certification requirement
Commerce	X	X
DOD	X	X
HHS		
DHS		
Justice[a]		
DOT		
Treasury		
VA	X	

Source: GAO analysis of agency documentation and interviews.

[a]Although Justice does not have an agencywide training program, FBI has a training program for its special agent personnel, including those working in cybersecurity.

[40]GAO, *Human Capital: A Guide for Assessing Strategic Training and Development Efforts in the Federal Government*, GAO-04-546G (Washington D.C.: March 2004), and OPM, *Human Resources Flexibilities and Authorities in the Federal Government* (Washington, D.C.: January 2008).

Of the eight agencies we reviewed, three—Commerce, DOD, and VA—have departmentwide training programs for their cybersecurity workforce. Commerce and DOD also have certification requirements for cybersecurity positions. Specifically,

- In September 2010, Commerce established minimum training requirements for individuals in designated cybersecurity roles, and requires personnel in selected positions to hold relevant professional certifications. Commerce's Office of the CIO did not provide data on the number of individuals covered by this policy, although one official reported that in 2011, 40 employees were participating in its Cybersecurity Development Program, which prepares participants for certification.

- DOD's Information Assurance Workforce Improvement Program sets training and certification requirements for all agency personnel who perform information assurance functions, regardless of whether information assurance is an employee's primary duty. The program covered approximately 88,000 people as of calendar year 2010. Between fiscal years 2007 and 2011, DOD allocated more than $53 million to cover the cost of certifications and certification membership fees for the program, not including additional funds DOD components may have expended to support the program's execution. DOD officials said they found the certification requirement valuable based on feedback from DOD components. As an example of the benefits of the program, the department reported reductions in the number of identified vulnerabilities at a military command as the number of trained and certified employees increased. DOD further noted that it found the requirement for certificate owners to participate in continuing education to be valuable for keeping the skills of its cybersecurity workforce up-to-date. In addition, NSA and other DOD components have their own specialized training programs for cybersecurity personnel, with requirements above and beyond those of DOD's Information Assurance Workforce Improvement Program.

- VA has a departmentwide training program that requires its information security officers to complete a 2-year training and mentoring program based on an internally-developed curriculum, which officials said resembles that of a private-sector professional certification. Participants are encouraged, but not required, to take the certification exam.

The remaining agencies do not have specific departmentwide cybersecurity training programs:

- The HHS Chief Information Security Officer reported that the agency budgets approximately $1,500 per cybersecurity employee for training and development activities and tailors individual development and training plans to employee needs, but does not have a structured training and development program for cybersecurity personnel.

- DHS officials reported that while it budgets $2,000 per person per year for training, the department does not have a specific training and development program for its cybersecurity personnel, though it is in the process of developing one.

- Justice officials said that while the department does not have a structured program for training cybersecurity personnel, it tailors employee individual development plans to meet the agency's needs. FBI, however, has a componentwide program providing specialized cybersecurity training tailored to its agents' skills in accordance with the component's missions and goals. In addition, Justice officials stated that while the training required to earn a certification may be valuable, the certification requirement itself was of limited additional value, and thus did not require certification for employees.

- DOT does not currently have a departmentwide training program for its cybersecurity staff, although it reported that some components have such programs. The department stated that its cybersecurity strategic plan calls for the department to create an agencywide program, but that limited funding has affected this goal.

- Treasury officials reported that its components are responsible for developing their own cybersecurity training programs, based on their own unique needs. Treasury's Chief Information Security Officer also said that in his opinion, commercial certifications were often too general to be applied to specific cybersecurity positions.

Multiple Governmentwide Efforts Under Way to Enhance Cybersecurity Workforce, but Efforts Lack Planning and Coordination

The federal government has begun several initiatives to enhance the federal cybersecurity workforce.

- The National Initiative for Cybersecurity Education (NICE) is an interagency effort coordinated by NIST to improve the nation's cybersecurity education, including efforts directed at the federal workforce. NIST has recently released a draft strategic plan for NICE for public comment, but the initiative lacks key details on activities to be accomplished and does not have clear authority to accomplish its goals.

- The CIO Council, NIST, OPM, and DHS all have separate efforts to develop a framework and models outlining cybersecurity roles, responsibilities, skills, and competencies. Officials reported plans to coordinate these efforts, but did not have specific time frames for doing so.

- The Information Systems Security Line of Business is a governmentwide initiative to create security training shared service centers. The effort is led by DHS and administered by DOD, the National Aeronautics and Space Administration (NASA), State, and VA. Each center offers cybersecurity training for use by other agencies, but there are currently no plans to coordinate the centers' offerings or gather feedback on the training or incorporate lessons learned into revisions of the training.

- The IT Workforce Capability Assessment, administered by the CIO Council, is an effort to gather data on governmentwide IT training needs, including cybersecurity. The assessment is to occur every 2 years, but the CIO Council has no specific plans to use the results of the assessments.

- DHS and NSF's Scholarship for Service program provides funding for undergraduate and graduate cybersecurity education in exchange for a commitment by recipients to work for the federal government. Most agencies we reviewed stated they believed the program was valuable. However, NSF currently does not track the longer-term value of the program by, for example, determining how many participants remain in government beyond their service commitment, but is working in an effort to develop and implement better ways to track this information.

NICE Has Recently Released a Draft Strategic Plan, but Lacks Governance Structure and Key Details on Achieving Goals

NICE began in March 2010 as an expansion of Initiative 8 of the Comprehensive National Cybersecurity Initiative, which focused on efforts to educate and improve the federal cybersecurity workforce.[41] According to the interagency committee recommendations establishing NICE, it is to provide program management support and promote intergovernmental efforts to improve cybersecurity awareness, education, workforce structure, and training. According to officials coordinating NICE activities, the efforts accomplished as part of the initiative include incorporating the Federal Information Systems Security Educators' Association[42] into NICE, launching the pilot of a virtual training environment for federal cybersecurity education, and releasing OPM's cybersecurity competency model.

In August 2011, NIST released a draft strategic plan for NICE, which provides high-level goals and a mission and vision. (See table 9.) Specifically, the plan states that the mission is to enhance the overall cybersecurity posture of the United States by accelerating the availability of educational and training resources designed to improve the cyber behavior, skills, and knowledge of every segment of the population. Activities to develop the federal cybersecurity workforce are contained under broader national workforce development efforts as part of the third NICE goal described in table 9.

---

[41] In January 2008, President Bush issued National Security Presidential Directive 54/Homeland Security Presidential Directive 23, establishing the Comprehensive National Cybersecurity Initiative, a set of projects aimed at safeguarding executive branch information systems by reducing potential vulnerabilities, protecting against intrusion attempts, and anticipating future threats.

[42] The Federal Information Systems Security Educators' Association is an organization of federal information systems security professionals that provides a forum for the exchange of information on federal information systems security awareness, training, and education programs.

Table 9: Goals of NICE

Goal	Participants	Description
1. Raise awareness about risks of online activities	DOD, DHS, Department of Education, NIST, NSF	A national cybersecurity awareness campaign intended to raise public awareness about the risks of online activities at home, in the workplace, and in communities.
2. Broaden the pool of skilled workers capable of supporting a cyber-secure nation	DHS, Department of Education, NIST, NSF, NSA	A set of programs intended to strengthen the pipeline of federal and private sector workers by bolstering formal cybersecurity education programs in kindergarten through 12th grade, with a focus on science, technology, engineering, and mathematics education.
3. Develop and maintain an unrivaled, globally competitive cybersecurity workforce	DOD, DHS, Department of Education, NIST, NSF, NSA, OPM	A series of efforts directed at workforce planning, professional development, and the identification of core professional competencies for the cybersecurity workforce, including the federal cybersecurity workforce. These efforts are directed at identifying and documenting skills, competencies, and the training necessary for the cybersecurity workforce to be effective.

Source: GAO analysis of NIST documentation.

While the NICE strategic plan describes several ambitious outcomes, the departments involved in NICE have not developed details on how they are going to achieve the outcomes. For example, the plan states that cybersecurity training will be aligned and integrated at all levels, federal agencies' human resources guidance should address cybersecurity work by 2013, and the workplace will see a 20-percent increase in qualified cybersecurity professionals by 2015. However, neither NICE nor participating agencies have released supporting plans to achieve these outcomes, such as current baseline information, needed resources, subtasks, and intermediate milestones.

Specific tasks under and responsibilities for NICE activities are also unclear. For example, the NICE strategic plan mentions the three goals listed in the previous table. Other NICE documentation refers to four components, each led by multiple agencies, that are similar to the goals. Furthermore, no comprehensive list of specific agency initiatives that are considered part of NICE has been published, and while NIST officials stated that each outcome listed in the strategic plan is based on input from a particular federal agency, the agency is not listed in the strategic plan, making it difficult to determine responsibility for the outcome.

Furthermore, NICE lacks a clear governance structure. According to NIST officials involved in NICE, specific initiatives under NICE are the responsibility of individual agencies, and those agencies will need to develop more detailed implementation plans. However, no time frame was provided for these plans to be developed. According to NIST officials coordinating NICE activities, NICE is primarily a consensus-driven group without a formal governance structure, and does not have authority to create or enforce goals or targets for individual agency activities. The officials also stated that the draft strategic plan would be revised based on public comments, but did not provide a deadline for its release.

Results-oriented strategic planning provides organizations with a set of performance goals for which they will be held accountable, measures progress toward those goals, determines strategies and resources to effectively accomplish the goals, uses performance information to make the programmatic decisions necessary to improve performance, and formally communicates the results in performance reports.

The lack of a clear governance structure and finalized and detailed plans means that the ability of NICE to achieve any of its goals, including those directed at the federal workforce, may be limited. Since NICE is an interagency working group with limited authority over its component organizations, clear governance, goals, milestones, and assignment of resources could help to ensure that the initiative performs as intended.

The CIO Council, NIST, OPM, and DHS Have All Taken Steps to Define Cybersecurity Roles and Competencies

To assist agencies, the CIO Council, NIST, OPM, and DHS have all engaged in separate efforts intended to help agencies define roles, responsibilities, skills, and competencies for their cybersecurity workforce.

CIO Council Is Developing Matrices to Identify Needed Cybersecurity Skills and Knowledge

In October 2010, the CIO Council released an updated version of 11 standard cybersecurity roles that agencies could use as a guideline in developing detailed position descriptions and training. (See table 10.)

Table 10: Information Security Roles as defined by the CIO Council

Role	Definition
Chief information officer	Focuses on information security strategy within an organization and is responsible for the strategic use and management of information, information systems, and IT.
Chief information security officer	Establishes, implements, and monitors the development and subsequent enforcement of the organization's information security program.
Digital forensics and incident response analyst	Performs a variety of highly technical analyses and procedures dealing with the collection, processing, preservation, analysis, and presentation of computer-related evidence, and is responsble for disseminating and reporting cyber-related activities, conducting vulnerability analyses, and risk management of computer systems and all applications during all phases of the system development life cycle.
Information security assessor	Oversees, participates in evaluating, and supports compliance issues pertinent to the organization.
Information security risk analyst	Facilitates and develops data-gathering methods to control and minimize risks by understanding external threats and vulnerabilities to the operation and environment.
Information systems security officer	Specializes in the information and security strategy within a system and is engaged throughout the systems development life cycle.
Information security systems and software development specialist	Securely designs, develops, tests, integrates, implements, maintains, or documents software applications (Web-based and non-Web), following formal secure systems development life cycle processes and using security engineering principles.
Network security specialist	Examines malicious software, suspicious network activities, and nonauthorized presence in the network to analyze the nature of a threat, and to secure and monitor firewall configurations.
Security architect	Implements business needs. Supports the business function as well as technology and environmental conditions (e.g., law and regulation), and translates them into security designs that support the organization to efficiently carry out its activities while minimizing risks from security threats and vulnerabilities.
Systems operations and maintenance professional	Supports and implements the security of information and information systems during the operations, maintenance, and enhancements phases of the systems development life cycle.
Vulnerability analyst	Detects threats and vulnerabilities in target systems, networks, and applications by conducting systems, network, and Web penetration testing.

Source: GAO analysis of CIO Council matrices.

For each role, the CIO Council plans to develop a workforce development matrix that lists suggestions for

- qualifications for entry, intermediate, and advanced performance levels for the role;

- additional sources for skill and competency materials;

- educational and professional credentials; and

- learning and development sources.

As of August 2011, the council had developed detailed matrices for four roles: chief information security officer, information security assessor, information security systems and software development professional, and systems operations and maintenance professional, and had drafted two additional matrices, for information systems security professional and information security auditor, which have not yet been released.

NIST Guidelines Outline Cybersecurity Responsibilities Related to FISMA

As part of its responsibilities under FISMA, NIST has defined cybersecurity roles and responsibilities in the following publications:[43]

- Special Publication 800-16, *Information Security Training Requirements: A Role-and Performance-Based Model* (draft);

- Special Publication 800-37, *Guide for Applying the Risk Management Framework to Federal Information Systems*; and

- Special Publication 800-50, *Building an Information Technology Security Awareness and Training Program.*

Table 11 identifies the cybersecurity roles defined in each publication.

---

[43]NIST Special Publication 800-37 Revision 1; Special Publication 800-16 Revision 1, *Information Security Training Requirements: A Role-and Performance-Based Model* (draft) (Gaithersburg, Md.: 2009); Special Publication 800-50, *Building an Information Technology Security Awareness and Training Program* (Gaithersburg, Md.: 2003).

Table 11: Information Security Roles as defined by NIST Special Publications

Role	Definition	800-16	800-37	800-50
Head of agency (chief executive officer)	The highest-level senior official or executive within an organization with the overall responsibility to provide information security protections commensurate with the risk and magnitude of harm (i.e., impact) to organizational operations and assets, individuals, other organizations.	X	X	X
Chief information officer	Performs a variety of duties including developing and maintaining information security policies, procedures, and control techniques to address all applicable requirements; overseeing personnel with significant responsibilities for information security and ensuring that the personnel are adequately trained; assisting senior organizational officials concerning their security responsibilities; and coordinating with other senior officials.	X	X	X
Risk executive	Helps to ensure that risk-related considerations for individual information systems, to include authorization decisions, are viewed from an organizationwide perspective with regard to the overall strategic goals and objectives of the organization in carrying out its core missions and business functions and that information system-related security risks are consistent across the organization.		X	
Information owner/steward	Responsible for establishing the policies and procedures governing the generation, collection, processing, dissemination, and disposal of information.		X	
Senior information security officer	Carries out the chief information officer security responsibilities under FISMA and serves as the primary liaison for the chief information officer to the organization's authorizing officials, information system owners, common control providers, and information system security officers.		X	
Senior agency information security officer	Responsible for the organization's information security awareness and training program.	X		
Authorizing official	Senior official or executive with the authority to formally assume responsibility for operating an information system at an acceptable level of risk to organizational operations and assets, individuals, other organizations, and the nation.		X	
Authorizing official designated representative	An organizational official that acts on behalf of an authorizing official to coordinate and conduct the required day-to-day activities associated with the security authorization process.		X	
Common control provider	Responsible for the development, implementation, assessment, and monitoring of common controls.		X	
Information system owner	Responsible for the procurement, development, integration, modification, operation, maintenance, and disposal of an information system.		X	
Information system security officer	Ensures that the appropriate operational security posture is maintained for an information system and as such, works in close collaboration with the information system owner.		X	
Information security architect	Ensures that the information security requirements necessary to protect the organization's core missions and business processes are adequately addressed in all aspects of enterprise architecture including reference models, segment and solution architectures, and the resulting information systems supporting those missions and business processes.		X	
Information system security engineer	Captures and refines information security requirements and ensures that the requirements are effectively integrated into IT component products and information systems through security architecture, design, development, and configuration.		X	

Role	Definition	800-16	800-37	800-50
Security control assessor	Conducts a comprehensive assessment of the management, operational, and technical security controls employed within or inherited by an information system to determine the overall effectiveness of the controls.		X	
IT security program manager	Responsible for the information security awareness and training program.			X
Managers	Responsible for complying with information security awareness, awareness training, and role-based training requirements established for their employees, users, and those who have been identified as having significant responsibilities for information security.	X		X
Instructional design specialists	Develops information security awareness training and role-based courses.	X		
Personnel with significant responsibilities for information security	Personnel who should understand that information security is an integral part of their job; what the organization expects of them; how to implement and maintain information security controls; mitigate risk to information and information systems; monitor the security condition of the security program, system, application, or information for which they are responsible; or what to do when security breaches are discovered.	X		
Users	Largest audience in any organization and the single most important group of people who can help reduce unintentional errors and related information system vulnerabilities.	X		X

Source: GAO summary of NIST publications.

As previously discussed, some of the roles in the NIST guidance map to roles the CIO Council has defined, while others do not. As of August 2011, NIST did not indicate plans to align the roles identified in NIST publications with the CIO Council roles. According to the agency, the roles are based on NIST's responsibilities under FISMA, and as such, do not need to be revised to align with the CIO Council roles. However, providing multiple unaligned sources of guidance to federal agencies limits the value of the guidance as a tool for agencies to use.

OPM Has Developed a Competency Model for Cybersecurity, but Has No Plans to Track Use or Revise

In 2009, OPM, in coordination with the CIO Council and a subcommittee of the Chief Human Capital Officers Council, identified cybersecurity as a high priority for developing a governmentwide cybersecurity competency model. As a part of this effort, OPM convened a series of focus groups to help develop a survey that was distributed in 2010 to cybersecurity professionals across the federal government. The survey, which was released in February 2011, was used to develop a competency model for the four most common job series used by cybersecurity professionals.[44]

---

[44]The series were 2210, Information Technology Management; 0855, Electrical Engineering; 0854, Computer Engineering; and 0391, Telecommunications Engineering.

The five competencies that were identified by the model as most important for cybersecurity professionals are listed in table 12.

Table 12: Top Five Competencies Identified by OPM's Cybersecurity Competency Model

Competency	Description
Integrity/honesty	Contr butes to maintaining the integrity of the organization; displays high standards of ethical conduct and understands the impact of violating these standards on an organization, self, and others; is trustworthy.
Computer skills	Uses computers, software applications, databases, and automated systems to accomplish work.
Technical competence	Uses knowledge that is acquired through formal training or extensive on-the-job experience to perform one's job; works with, understands, and evaluates technical information related to the job; advises others on technical issues.
Teamwork	Encourages and facilitates cooperation, pride, trust, and group identity; fosters commitment and team spirit; works with others to achieve goals.
Attention to detail	Is thorough when performing work and conscientious about attending to detail.

Source: OPM competency model.

Future adoption of the model may be limited for several reasons. First, the competency model is dominated by competencies that are not unique to cybersecurity. None of the top five competencies that are identified as important are specific to cybersecurity work. OPM officials stated that the "technical competence" competency could be further defined by an agency with specific cybersecurity skills for a particular position. Second, adoption of the cybersecurity workforce competency model is optional for agencies. OPM does not plan to track usage of the competency model by individual agencies, nor does it plan to collect feedback on the usefulness of the model or update it.

OPM officials stated that they believe the cybersecurity competency model will be adopted throughout the federal government. However, until OPM tracks usage of the competency model, collects feedback on the model, and develops plans to update it in response to feedback, the usefulness of the model may be unknown.

DHS Is Developing a Framework to Characterize the National Cybersecurity Workforce, with Future Plans to Align Other Models and Frameworks

DHS is developing a framework supporting NICE that is intended to provide common language for describing the cybersecurity workforce. The framework consists of 31 specialties, spread across seven categories of cybersecurity work. The seven categories are listed in table 13.

Table 13: DHS/NICE Cybersecurity Framework Work Categories

Category	Description
Securely provision	Conceptualizing, designing, and building secure IT systems, with responsibility for some aspect of the systems' development.
Operate and maintain	Providing the support, administration, and maintenance necessary to ensure effective and efficient IT system performance and security.
Protect and defend	Identification, analysis, and mitigation of threats to internal IT systems or networks.
Investigate	Investigation of cyber events/crimes of IT systems, networks, and/or digital evidence.
Operate and collect	Highly specialized and largely classified collection of cybersecurity information that may be used to develop intelligence.
Analyze	Highly specialized and largely classified review and evaluation of incoming cybersecurity information to determine its usefulness for intelligence.
Support	Providing support so that others may effectively conduct their cybersecurity work.

Source: NICE.

For each specialty, DHS has developed a brief summary description of the specialty, a list of tasks performed by individuals in that specialty, and a list of knowledge, skills, and abilities someone in that specialty should have. The list maps to the technical competencies in OPM's cybersecurity competency model. A DHS official responsible for the framework stated that the draft framework was developed with input primarily from members of the intelligence community and DOD.

A draft of the framework was released for public comment in September 2011. DHS reports it is seeking input from academia, cybersecurity organizations, and the private sector as it continues to develop and refine the framework.

According to DHS's Director of National Cybersecurity Education Strategy, once the DHS/NICE framework has been finalized, other federal documents, including NIST Special Publication 800-16 and the document governing DOD's Information Assurance Workforce Improvement Program, among others, will be rewritten to conform to it, but she did not provide a time frame for this to occur.

CIO Council, OPM, and DHS Report Plans to Coordinate Efforts, but Lack Specific Time Frames

While officials with the CIO Council, OPM, and DHS reported that steps are being taken to coordinate their various efforts related to defining the cybersecurity workforce, at the moment, each one, along with existing NIST guidelines, takes a different approach, using different categorizations of roles and terminology. The CIO Council's Workforce Development Matrices use roles, performance levels, competencies, skills, suggested credentials, and suggested training; NIST guidelines are based on FISMA-related responsibilities; OPM's competency model addresses cybersecurity professionals in terms of series, grade, and competencies; and the DHS/NICE framework uses work categories, specialties, tasks, and knowledge, skills, and abilities. According to CIO Council representatives responsible for developing the matrices and NICE officials, the matrices, frameworks, and special publication were developed from different perspectives, but the officials acknowledged that in future versions they could be better aligned. Officials did not identify any specific time frames for these activities.

While NIST guidelines are already widely used throughout the federal government, there are currently no specific steps to promote the use of the other efforts' products governmentwide. OPM officials have stated that agency use of its competency model is voluntary, and representatives of the CIO Council and NICE have all stated they have no authority to require federal agencies to make use of their products, and did not identify specific steps they were taking to promote their use in the federal government. The DHS official responsible for development of the DHS/NICE framework stated other relevant documents would be rewritten to conform to the framework, but the NICE lead at NIST stated that NICE can only build consensus, not mandate standards.

The CIO Council, NIST, OPM, and DHS/NICE efforts could help individual agencies in their own workforce planning efforts, reducing the amount of work each agency may have to do on its own. However, having multiple entities develop similar role and competency models is not an efficient use of resources. We have previously reported[45] that reducing or eliminating duplication in government programs could save billions of tax dollars annually and help agencies provide more efficient services. Until these organizations take steps to consolidate and better coordinate their efforts, it is unlikely that any of these efforts will be able to maximize its effectiveness, or that agencies will be able to reconcile their roles and responsibilities in an efficient and effective manner.

---

[45]GAO, *Opportunities to Reduce Potential Duplication in Government Programs, Save Tax Dollars, and Enhance Revenue*, GAO-11-318SP (Washington, D.C.: Mar. 1, 2011).

Information Systems Security Line of Business Has Multiple Providers for Cybersecurity Training, but Training Efforts Are Not Coordinated or Evaluated by DHS

In 2005, OMB and DHS collaborated on an initiative, called the Information Systems Security Line of Business, to address common information systems security needs across the government, including cybersecurity training. DHS authorized five agencies to be security training shared service centers available to all federal agencies so as to reduce duplication and improve the quality of information security training. The training courses that they offer are organized into two training tiers: general security awareness training and role-based security training, which is offered by four of the five agencies, specifically State, DOD, NASA, and VA. The role-based security training is focused on individuals who perform significant cybersecurity tasks as part of their job. Agencies are required by FISMA to ensure that these individuals receive appropriate training for those tasks. The status of the training provided by each shared service center follows.

State/DOD

State is involved in a pilot effort, sponsored by DHS, to deliver online role-based cybersecurity training to up to 125,000 federal employees, called the Federal Virtual Training Environment (FedVTE). FedVTE includes content from DOD's role-based training. State reported that the environment currently holds about 800 hours of recorded classroom training and over 75 hands-on labs. The agency also stated that a phased rollout of FedVTE is planned to begin in the second quarter of fiscal year 2012 contingent on the successful completion of the pilot. A companion program, the Federal Cybersecurity Training Exercise (FedCTE), is also being developed. FedCTE supplements the online FedVTE training with in-person training.

NASA

NASA offers cybersecurity training for nine cybersecurity roles, such as system administrator and chief information officer, and makes the training available at no charge to other agencies on compact disc. This training was developed for use at NASA, and the role-based training courses were developed for NASA purposes. NASA officials stated that the training is customizable, but they do not provide support in customizing the courses for use by other federal agencies.

VA

VA has developed training for nine roles, and has made them available to other federal agencies through Web-based training. The courses cover topics such as fundamentals of cybersecurity, FISMA controls and reporting, and system certification and accreditation. VA officials stated that while they have an interest in customizing the training to support other agencies, they currently do not have a process in place to do so. For example, the agency does not have a means of accepting reimbursement for the costs of customization.

In order to build the capacity they need to achieve their missions and goals, federal agencies need to make wise decisions when investing in training and development programs for their workforce. We have previously reported[46] that agencies need to evaluate their training programs to ensure that they are successfully enhancing the skills and competencies of their employees and that reducing or eliminating duplication in government programs could save billions of tax dollars annually and help agencies provide more efficient services.[47]

While one of the goals of the shared program is to reduce duplication, there are several areas in which the training roles overlap among the agencies, and no process exists for coordinating or eliminating duplication among the efforts. For example, NASA, VA, and State all have training for employees in system administrator roles. Additionally, both NASA and VA offer training for CIOs, and NASA and State both offer training directed at the system owner role. As a result, an increased risk exists that training providers are offering duplicative training. DHS officials stated they are just starting to consider better coordination of the training centers, but did not have a specific plan for doing so. Reducing or eliminating duplication and overlap among the shared service providers would allow for more efficient and effective training to be offered by each agency, and could allow for a greater amount of training and broader range of courses to be provided at the same expense.

Additionally, DHS does not have, and does not require training providers to offer, a mechanism for gathering feedback on training and incorporating lessons learned into revisions, so there are no data available on how useful the current training is or means to compare the training of the different providers. DHS stated that it did not have authority

---

[46]GAO, *Human Capital: Selected Agencies' Experiences and Lessons Learned in Designing Training and Development Programs*, GAO-04-291 (Washington, D.C.: Jan. 30, 2004).

[47]GAO-11-318SP.

to require training providers to gather feedback or incorporate lessons learned into the training provided. However, soliciting and acting on feedback could provide a means for the training offerings to be more effective and more broadly used.

CIO Council's IT Workforce Capability Assessment Revealed Governmentwide Cybersecurity Training Needs

The IT Workforce Capability Assessment is an effort by the CIO Council to gather data on the training needs of the federal IT workforce, including those who work in cybersecurity. The assessment, which stems in part from a requirement in the Clinger-Cohen Act that agencies assess the training needs of their IT staff, was originally intended to be an annual effort and was first conducted in 2003.[48] However, according to officials responsible for the effort, because of budget limitations, it was not conducted again until 2006 and then again in 2011.

The CIO Council stated that participating agencies are to use the agency-level data to support their workforce planning efforts and the aggregate data to provide an overall snapshot of the capabilities and skills of the federal IT workforce. In June, the CIO Council released the results of this year's assessment, which included for the first time a supplemental assessment of the cybersecurity workforce. Survey participants who indicated they perform cybersecurity activities were asked to rate their proficiency on the cybersecurity technical competencies identified in OPM's cybersecurity competency model and to identify competencies in which they and their organizations could benefit from training. About 42 percent of the approximately 18,000 survey respondents identified themselves as performing cybersecurity work. These participants rated their proficiency in the technical competencies identified in OPM's cybersecurity competency model on a five-point scale, and also identified competencies in which they and their organizations needed additional training.

Training in forensics and vulnerabilities assessment topped the list of individual and organizational training needs, according to the survey results. Tables 14 and 15 detail the top five individual and organizational training needs, respectively.

---

[48] 40 U.S.C. § 11315(c)(3).

Table 14: Top Five Individual Cybersecurity Competency Training Needs

Individual training need	Number of respondents	Percentage of total
Forensics	3,306	44.4
Computer network defense	3,193	42.9
Vulnerabilities assessment	2,952	39.6
Communications security management	2,093	28.1
Incident management	1,852	24.9

Source: CIO Council reported survey responses.

Table 15: Top Five Organizational Cybersecurity Competency Training Needs

Organizational training need	Number of respondents	Percentage of total
Vulnerabilities assessment	2,607	35.8
Computer network defense	2,407	32.3
Compliance	2,146	28.8
Communications security management	2,054	27.6
Incident management	1,920	25.8

Source: CIO Council reported survey responses.

While current plans are for the assessment to be conducted every 2 years, of the eight agencies we reviewed, only DOD and DHS identified specific plans to use the assessment data. Furthermore, the CIO Council does not have any specific plans for the use of the governmentwide survey data. We have previously identified surveys as a useful tool for gathering information on employee skills and training needs,[49] but unless this information is used to inform training and development efforts, the effort spent gathering it will likely be wasted. Accordingly, unless the assessment results are integrated into existing agency and governmentwide workforce planning and training activities, their value is limited.

---

[49]GAO-04-291.

Scholarship for Service Program Produces Skilled Cybersecurity Workers, but Long-Term Retention in Government Is Unknown

The Scholarship for Service (SFS) program, cosponsored by NSF and DHS, provides scholarships and stipends to undergraduate and graduate students who are pursuing information security-related degrees. In exchange for this financial support, the student must agree to work in an IT internship with the federal government while in school and to take a full-time cybersecurity position with the government after graduation for up to 2 years. In calendar years 2009 and 2010, the SFS program produced 203 graduates, of which approximately 95 percent had secured a cybersecurity position with the government as of December 2010. DOD and its components hired 49 percent of the program's graduates in that period, with 24 percent going to NSA, and the remaining 25 percent being hired by the military services and the civilian DOD. According to NSF, the program costs approximately $14 million per year.

Most of the agencies we talked with stated that the SFS program is a valuable resource for recruiting cybersecurity professionals; however, it is a relatively small program, graduating approximately 125 to 150 cybersecurity students each year. This number, when spread across 24 major federal agencies, does not provide a significant number of cybersecurity workers to meet the needs of the federal government.

It is also unclear how many of these students remain in federal service after their service repayment period has been fulfilled. An NSF official responsible for the program stated that it is difficult to track the retention rate of the students after their fulfillment is completed and that the agency has no accurate way of knowing how many students stay in the federal government. The official noted that the agency is currently working with two different groups in an effort to develop and implement better ways to track the students that are in repayment to determine whether they remain in federal work (including employment at intelligence agencies) after their contractual obligations have been completed. Until NSF develops and establishes effective tracking mechanisms to capture the retention rates of students beyond their contractual obligations, it is unclear how beneficial the program is in relation to other federal cybersecurity workforce development activities.

Conclusions

Federal agencies vary in their implementation of planning practices for their cybersecurity workforce. Five agencies have addressed several key principles in their workforce plans, but three agencies did not have any workforce plans that addressed cybersecurity needs. A challenge in cybersecurity workforce planning is the difficulty in defining and identifying cybersecurity workers. Further, many agencies have taken steps to define cybersecurity roles, responsibilities, skills, and competencies, but are hampered by the inconsistent alignment of existing governmentwide guidance. Agencies reported mixed results in filling cybersecurity positions, with specific challenges in filling highly technical positions and with hiring and security clearance processes, but are taking steps to address these challenges. Use of incentives for cybersecurity positions varied widely by agency, with DOD offering the widest range of incentives. However, no data exist on the effectiveness of incentives, in part because of the lack of guidance on tracking such data from OPM. Differences in compensation systems also affected agency perceptions of their ability to recruit cybersecurity personnel. Training and development opportunities also vary widely at agencies.

Several governmentwide efforts to improve cybersecurity workforce planning activities are under way, but NICE, which is intended to promote governmentwide cybersecurity efforts, lacks finalized and detailed plans needed to help ensure its goals are achieved. Multiple efforts by the CIO Council, NIST, OPM, and DHS have defined cybersecurity roles, responsibilities, skills, and competencies, but these efforts are potentially duplicative and could be better coordinated. Similarly, multiple efforts to assess and provide training needs are under way, but lack coordination. In an era of limited financial resources, better coordinated efforts to address both cybersecurity-specific and broader federal workforce challenges are crucial to cost-effectively ensuring that the government has the people it needs to continue to deal with evolving cyber threats.

Recommendations for Executive Action

To improve individual agency cybersecurity workforce planning efforts, we are making the following recommendations:

- We recommend that the Secretary of Commerce direct the department's Chief Information Officer, in consultation with its Chief Human Capital Officer, to develop and implement a departmentwide cybersecurity workforce plan or ensure that departmental components are conducting appropriate workforce planning activities.

- We recommend that the Secretary of Defense direct the department's Chief Information Officer, in consultation with the Deputy Assistant Secretary for Defense for Civilian Personnel Policy, to update its departmentwide cybersecurity workforce plan or ensure that departmental components have plans that appropriately address human capital approaches, critical skills, competencies, and supporting requirements for its cybersecurity workforce strategies.

- We recommend that the Secretary of Health and Human Services direct the department's Chief Information Officer, in consultation with its Chief Human Capital Officer, to develop and implement a departmentwide cybersecurity workforce plan or ensure that departmental components are conducting appropriate workforce planning activities.

- We recommend that the Secretary of Transportation direct the department's Chief Information Officer, in consultation with its Chief Human Capital Officer, to update its departmentwide cybersecurity workforce plan or ensure that departmental components have plans that fully address gaps in human capital approaches and critical skills and competencies and supporting requirements for its cybersecurity workforce strategies.

- We recommend that the Secretary of Treasury direct the department's Chief Information Officer, in consultation with its Chief Human Capital Officer, to develop and implement a departmentwide cybersecurity workforce plan or ensure that departmental components are conducting appropriate workforce planning activities.

- We recommend that the Secretary of Veterans Affairs direct the department's Chief Information Officer, in consultation with its Chief Human Capital Officer, to update its departmentwide cybersecurity competency model or establish a cybersecurity workforce plan that fully addresses gaps in human capital approaches and critical skills and competencies, supporting requirements for its cybersecurity workforce strategies, and monitoring and evaluating agency progress.

To help federal agencies better identify their cybersecurity workforce, we recommend the Director of the Office of Personnel Management, in coordination with the Director of the Office of Management and Budget, collaborate with the CIO Council to identify and develop governmentwide strategies to address challenges federal agencies face in tracking their cybersecurity workforce.

To ensure that governmentwide cybersecurity workforce initiatives are better coordinated and planned, and to better assist federal agencies in defining roles, responsibilities, skills, and competencies for their workforce, we recommend that the Secretary of Commerce, Director of the Office of Management and Budget, Director of the Office of Personnel

Management, and Secretary of Homeland Security collaborate through the NICE initiative to take the following three actions:

- clarify the governance structure for NICE to specify responsibilities and processes for planning and monitoring of initiative activities;

- develop and finalize detailed plans allowing agency accountability, measurement of progress, and determination of resources to accomplish agreed-upon activities; and

- consolidate and align efforts to define roles, responsibilities, skills, and competencies for the federal cybersecurity workforce.

To improve governmentwide cybersecurity workforce planning efforts, we recommend the Director of the Office of Personnel Management take the following actions:

- finalize and issue guidance to agencies on how to track the use and effectiveness of incentives for hard-to-fill positions, including cybersecurity positions and

- maximize the value of the cybersecurity competency model by (1) developing and implementing a method for ensuring that the competency model accurately reflects the skill set unique to the cybersecurity workforce, (2) developing a method for collecting and tracking data on the use of the competency model, and (3) creating a schedule for revising or updating the model as needed.

To improve governmentwide cybersecurity workforce planning efforts, we recommend that the Director of the Office of Management and Budget direct the CIO Council to develop a strategy for and track agencies' use of the IT Workforce Capability Assessment data.

To ensure that the benefits of the training provided through the Information Systems Security Line of Business are maximized, and resources are used most efficiently, we recommend the Secretary of the Department of Homeland Security take the following two actions:

- implement a process for tracking agency use of line of business training and gathering feedback from agencies on the training's value and opportunities for improvement and

- develop a process to coordinate training offered through the line of business to minimize the production and distribution of duplicative products.

To better determine the value to the government of the Scholarship for Service program, we recommend that the Director of the National Science Foundation develop and implement a mechanism to track the retention rate of program participants beyond their contractual obligation to the government.

Agency Comments and Our Evaluation

We provided a draft of this report to the agencies in our review. Of the six agencies to which we made individual recommendations regarding their workforce planning activities, five concurred and one agency neither concurred nor nonconcurred with our recommendations. A summary of comments follow.

- The Secretary of Commerce provided written comments in which the department generally concurred with our recommendation that it develop and implement a departmentwide cybersecurity workforce plan or ensure that departmental components are conducting appropriate workforce planning activities (Commerce's comments are reprinted in app. II).

- The Acting Assistant Secretary of Defense for Networks and Information Integration/DOD CIO provided written comments in which the department concurred with our recommendation that it update its departmentwide cybersecurity workforce plan or ensure that departmental components have plans that appropriately address human capital approaches, critical skills, competencies, and supporting requirements for cybersecurity workforce strategies (see app. III). The draft version of this report contained an additional recommendation to DOD regarding the agency's certification program. Based on additional discussions with the department, we have deleted this recommendation.

- The Assistant Secretary for Legislation for the Department of Health and Human Services provided written comments in which the department concurred with our recommendation to develop and implement a departmentwide cybersecurity workforce plan or ensure that departmental components are conducting appropriate workforce planning activities and stated that the Office of the Chief Information Officer will coordinate with the Office of Human Resources to

accomplish this with a target completion date of July 2012
(see app. V).

- The Deputy Director of Audit Relations for the Department of Transportation stated in oral comments that the department would not be providing formal written comments on our report and neither concurred nor nonconcurred with our recommendation to update its departmentwide cybersecurity workforce plan or ensure that departmental components have plans to address gaps in human capital approaches and critical skills and competencies and supporting requirements for its cybersecurity workforce strategies.

- The Deputy Assistant Secretary for Information Systems and Chief Information Officer for the Department of the Treasury provided written comments in which the department concurred with our recommendation to develop and implement a departmentwide cybersecurity workforce plan or ensure that departmental components are conducting appropriate workforce planning activities and stated that instructions will be issued to Treasury components requiring them to develop and submit plans to the department for evaluation and feedback (see app. VI).

- The Chief of Staff for the Department of Veterans Affairs provided written comments in which the department concurred with our recommendation to update its departmentwide cybersecurity competency model or establish a cybersecurity workforce plan that fully addresses gaps in human capital approaches and critical skills and competencies and supporting requirements for its cybersecurity workforce strategies, and stated that the Chief Information Officer and Chief Human Capital Officer will create and monitor an updated departmentwide cybersecurity workforce plan that addresses all noted deficiencies in a phased approach with a target completion date of January 30, 2013 (see app. VII).

Of the five agencies to which we made recommendations to address governmentwide challenges, four agencies—Commerce, DHS, OPM, and NSF—provided written comments on our recommendations. OMB did not provide written comments, but the OMB audit liaison did provide suggestions regarding the wording of our recommendations via e-mail, which we have considered. A summary of the responses from the four agencies follows.

- With respect to our recommendation to OMB and OPM to improve tracking of the federal cybersecurity workforce, the Associate Director

GAO-12-8 Cybersecurity Human Capital

of OPM Employee Services stated that the department concurred with our recommendation and that OPM will develop a data element for tracking the cybersecurity workforce in its Enterprise Human Resource Integration system and collaborate with the CIO Council, OMB, and other agencies as needed (see app. VIII).

- With respect to our recommendation to Commerce, DHS, OMB, and OPM to clarify the governance structure and develop and finalize detailed plans for NICE, and to consolidate and align efforts to define roles, responsibilities, skills, and competencies for the federal cybersecurity workforce, agencies provided the following comments:

  - The Secretary of Commerce concurred with our recommendation and outlined steps NIST is taking with other NICE components to develop more detailed plans for NICE activities.

  - The Director of DHS's Departmental GAO-OIG Liaison Office concurred with our recommendation and stated that the department will coordinate with its NICE counterparts to document the existing governance structure, ensure a system for accountability, and define federal cybersecurity workforce roles, responsibilities, skills, and competencies (see app. IV). In oral comments, DHS officials stated the importance of NICE components agreeing to undertake specific activities before more detailed plans could be developed.

  - The Associate Director of OPM Employee Services partially concurred with our recommendation on governance structure and developing and finalizing detailed plans, stating that it does not have the authority to implement recommendations involving NICE governance structure, and should be removed from this part of the recommendation. We acknowledge that NICE is a collaborative effort of multiple agencies. However, OPM does have key responsibilities for NICE, along with other federal agencies. As a result, we continue to address our recommendation regarding governance structure and plans to OPM together with Commerce, DHS, and OMB. We have clarified the wording of the recommendation to reflect our intent that this be a collaborative effort. The associate director concurred with our recommendation to consolidate and align efforts for federal cybersecurity workforce roles, responsibilities, skills and competencies.

- With respect to our recommendation to finalize and issue guidance to agencies on tracking the use and effectiveness of incentives, the

Associate Director of OPM Employee Services stated that the department concurred with our recommendation and identified steps OPM is taking to address federal agencies' use of incentives.

- The Associate Director of OPM Employee Services did not concur with our draft recommendation to maximize the value of OPM's cybersecurity competency model by ensuring its accuracy, tracking its use, and revising it on a regular basis. She stated that the agency's methodology for developing the model was consistent with legal and professional guidelines, that use of the model is optional, and that OPM is working with OMB to reduce human capital reporting requirements, rather than establishing new requirements. However, during our review, OPM was unable to demonstrate the extent to which agencies were using the cybersecurity competency model. Given that none of the competencies identified by the model as being most important are specific to cybersecurity, following up with agencies to see if the model is actually used and if it needs revision is important. Thus, we believe that the components of our recommendation to ensure the model accurately reflects the skill sets unique to the cybersecurity workforce and to track its use continue to have merit. The Associate Director also took exception with the component of our draft recommendation to create a schedule for revising or updating the model on a regular basis. She expressed concerns about the effort required for revising the model and indicated that models should be updated on an as-needed basis, rather than on an arbitrary timeline. We agree and have modified our recommendation accordingly.

- The Director of DHS's Departmental GAO-OIG Liaison Office concurred with our recommendations to DHS regarding improvements to the Information Systems Security Line of Business and stated that the department is developing a shared service center point of contact list for an annual data call for input toward future solutions to address our recommendation and will work with other shared service centers to ensure that they align with NICE activities and findings.

- The NSF Deputy Director concurred with our recommendation to develop a mechanism to track the retention rate of the Scholarship for Service program, but stated that our recommendation implied that the foundation was not planning to address this issue. The deputy director stated that the foundation is in the process of implementing a new monitoring and evaluation system to collect this type of data that will be operational in early 2012 (see app. IX).

Several agencies also provided technical comments that were incorporated into our report as appropriate.

We are sending copies of this report to the appropriate congressional committees; the Directors of OMB and NSF; the Secretaries of Commerce, Defense, Health and Human Services, Homeland Security, Transportation, Treasury, and Veterans Affairs; the Attorney General; and other interested congressional parties. The report also is available at no charge on the GAO website at http://www.gao.gov.

If you or your staff has any questions about this report, please contact Gregory Wilshusen at (202) 512-6244 or Valerie Melvin at (202) 512-6304, or by e-mail at wilshuseng@gao.gov or melvinv@gao.gov. Contact points for our Offices of Congressional Relations and Public Affairs may be found on the last page of this report. Key contributors to this report are listed in appendix X.

Gregory C. Wilshusen
Director,
Information Security Issues

Valerie C. Melvin
Director,
Information Management and Human Capital Issues

Appendix I: Objectives, Scope, and Methodology

The objectives of our review were to assess (1) the extent to which key federal agencies have implemented established workforce planning practices for cybersecurity personnel and (2) the status of and plans for governmentwide cybersecurity workforce initiatives.

The scope of our effort for the first objective was limited to the eight largest federal agencies based on information technology (IT) spending: the Departments of Defense (DOD), Homeland Security (DHS), Health and Human Services (HHS), Treasury, Veterans Affairs (VA), Commerce, Transportation (DOT), and Justice. We determined IT spending by using the average of spending estimates that federal agencies provided to the Office of Management and Budget (OMB) from fiscal year 2009 through fiscal year 2011.

To determine the extent to which these key federal agencies had implemented principles of workforce planning in their workforce plans, we compared each of the five GAO key principles that strategic workforce planning should address with the agencies' workforce plans. If the agencies' workforce plans fully addressed all of the elements under each principle, we considered the agency to have fully addressed the principle. If the agency addressed at least two elements of the principle, we considered the agency to have partially addressed the principle. We did not review the department's efforts to implement the key principles discussed in the workforce plans.

To determine the ability of agencies to determine the number of cybersecurity staff at the agency, we gathered data from OMB's 2010 report on the Federal Information Security Management Act (FISMA), data the Office of Personnel Management (OPM) provided that it had collected from its data gathering efforts with agencies, individual agency FISMA reports, and information provided directly from agencies on their cybersecurity workforce. We compared the data from the different sources, reviewed the data for obvious outliers and errors, and verified them with agency officials. We used this information to illustrate the problems with reliably identifying cybersecurity employees and determined it was sufficient for this purpose.

To assess agency definitions of roles and responsibilities and skills and competencies for cybersecurity staff, we analyzed agency policies and documentation, supplemented with interviews with agency officials, to determine the extent to which the agency had developed definitions based on either National Institute of Standards and Technology (NIST) or federal Chief Information Officers (CIO) Council guidelines. We

considered an agency to have partially developed roles and
responsibilities or skills and competencies if it had either only developed
selected definitions or had not implemented definitions across the entire
agency.

To determine the extent to which agencies had implemented additional
leading practices in workforce planning for cybersecurity personnel, we
reviewed our own guidance and reports on federal agencies' workforce
planning and human capital management efforts. We then analyzed
agency documentation related to its cybersecurity workforce, including
hiring and training plans, numbers of vacant and filled cybersecurity
positions, use of recruitment and retention incentives, and information on
salary structure and related personnel systems. We used this information
to determine the extent of each agency's efforts to identify critical
cybersecurity skills and competencies needed, challenges in developing
or obtaining these skills and competencies, and plans to address these
challenges based on leading practices in workforce planning. We also
compared the information across agencies to determine the level of
consistency. We supplemented the documentation provided by the
agencies with interviews we conducted with agency officials in information
security, training, and human resources.

To determine the status of governmentwide cybersecurity workforce
initiatives, we first identified governmentwide initiatives based on
interviews with subject matter experts at federal agencies and private
organizations, and a review of publicly released information on the
initiatives. For the initiatives identified, we reviewed plans, performance
measures, and status reports. We also interviewed officials at agencies
responsible for these initiatives, such as NIST, OPM, the National
Science Foundation, and OMB. We assessed the status and plans of
these efforts against our prior work on strategic planning, training and
development, and efficient government operations.

As part of our presentation of governmentwide cybersecurity workforce
initiatives, we presented the results of the IT Workforce Capability
Assessment administered by the CIO Council. While we did not
independently assess the quality of the survey and results, we examined
the data to identify any obvious problems with reasonableness and
accuracy, and discussed our presentation of the data with officials
responsible for the survey results. We determined these data were
sufficiently reliable for the purposes of this report.

We conducted this performance audit from December 2010 to November 2011 in accordance with generally accepted government auditing standards. Those standards require that we plan and perform the audit to obtain sufficient, appropriate evidence to provide a reasonable basis for our findings and conclusions based on our audit objectives. We believe that the evidence obtained provides a reasonable basis for our findings and conclusions based on our audit objectives.

Appendix II: Comments from the Department of Commerce

UNITED STATES DEPARTMENT OF COMMERCE
The Secretary of Commerce
Washington, D.C. 20230

October 28, 2011

Mr. Gregory C. Wilshusen
Director, Information Security Issues
U.S. Government Accountability Office
Washington, DC 20548

Dear Mr. Wilshusen:

Thank you for the opportunity to offer the Department of Commerce's comments on recommendations outlined by the U.S. Government Accountability Office (GAO) draft report entitled, *Cybersecurity Human Capital: Initiatives Need Better Planning and Coordination (GAO 12-8)*.

We generally concur with the report's recommendations regarding the Department's finding to develop and implement a department-wide cybersecurity workforce plan or ensure departmental components are conducting appropriate workforce planning activities. The Department's Chief Human Capital Officer will coordinate and/or delegate the responsibility to coordinate this effort to the Deputy Chief Human Capital Officer with support from the Chief Information Officer. We also concur with the report's recommendations regarding the National Initiative for Cybersecurity Education. We have provided attached additional comments regarding the draft report.

We welcome any further communication with GAO regarding its conclusions and look forward to receiving the final report. If you have any questions, please contact Tyra Dent Smith in the Office of the Chief Information Officer at (202) 482-4807.

Sincerely,

John E. Bryson

Enclosure

DEPARTMENT OF COMMERCE
COMMENTS ON GAO DRAFT REPORT
"Cybersecurity Human Capital: Initiatives Need Better Planning and Coordination (GAO 12-8)"

Regarding Table 2: *Comparison of Reported Number of Cybersecurity Workers from Multiple Sources* on Page 16 of the draft report, the Department recommends adding a note indicating that number provided under the "Personnel per GAO 2011 data call" column is based on Commerce information for only CIO organizations within the Department for significant security roles identified in the Commerce Interim Technical Requirement (CITR)-006 *Information System Security Training for Significant Roles.*

NIST's National Initiative for Cybersecurity Education (NICE)
COMMENTS ON GAO DRAFT REPORT
"Cybersecurity Human Capital: Initiatives Need Better Planning and Coordination (GAO 12-8)"

NIST concurs with the report whilst noting that many of the outcomes identified in the Recommendations for Executive Action are being addressed within the current governance structure of the National Initiative for Cybersecurity Education (NICE). NIST requests that "in coordination with NICE" be added to each recommendation to reflect the interagency partnership integral to the NICE structure.

Regarding GAO-12-8's focus on governance, NIST was designated as the lead for NICE by the Information and Communications Infrastructure – Interagency Policy Committee (ICI-IPC). As the designated lead, NIST is coordinating activities in cybersecurity education, training, and awareness to enhance and multiply their effectiveness. NICE is an interagency effort in which agencies identify common goals and milestones, commit their own resources toward achieving those goals, and align their respective implementation plans and activities. NICE's governance structure is comprised of the following four components:

- Component 1: National Cybersecurity Awareness Campaign led by the Department of Homeland Security (DHS).

- Component 2: Formal Cybersecurity Education led by the Department of Education (ED) and the National Science Foundation (NSF).

- Component 3: Cybersecurity Workforce Structure led by DHS and supported by the Office of Personnel Management (OPM). This component contains three Sub-Component Areas (SCAs); Federal Workforce, led by OPM; Government Workforce (non-Federal), led by DHS; Private Sector Workforce, led by Small Business Administration, Department of Labor, and NIST.

- Component 4: Cybersecurity Workforce Training and Development led by DHS, the
  Department of Defense (DoD) and the Office of the Director of National Intelligence
  (ODNI). This component contains four Functional Areas (FAs): General IT Use, led by
  DHS and Department of the Navy; IT Infrastructure, Operations, Maintenance &
  Information Assurance, led by DoD and DHS; Domestic Enforcement and
  Counterintelligence, led by Defense Cyber Crime Center, Office of the National
  Counterintelligence Executive, Department of Justice, and United States Secret Service;
  and Specialized Cybersecurity Operations, led by the National Security Agency.

Working from the current governance structure, NICE released for public comment a
draft strategic plan in August 2011 that describes NICE's major goals and objectives. The public
comments will be used to refine and finalize the Strategic Plan, which will guide the
development of annual program implementation plans. Annual program implementation plans
will be coordinated across all of the NICE agencies, holding agencies accountable to one
another, allowing measurement of progress, and documenting resource estimates to accomplish
its goals.

With regards to GAO-12-8's focus on the federal cybersecurity workforce, NICE has
developed a Cybersecurity Workforce Framework which identifies the various cybersecurity
functions, or specialty areas. Initially an outgrowth of DHS, DOD and ODNI studies, the
Framework has been shared for input with over 20 federal organizations, including the Federal
CIO council, as well as partners in academia, industry, non-federal governments, and
standardization and certification groups. To garner input from all sectors, it has recently been
posted for public comment.

The interagency partnership that guides the NICE initiative is common to many,
successful NIST activities. For example, GAO-12-8 references NIST Special Publication 800-37
(Guide for Applying the Risk Management Framework to Federal Information Systems). This
publication, which describes the roles and responsibilities of those involved in an organization's
risk management, was developed by the Joint Task Force Transformation Initiative Interagency
Working Group with representatives from the Civil, Defense, and Intelligence Communities in
an ongoing effort to produce a unified information security framework for the Federal
Government. NIST's extensive experience with coordinated interagency and public/private
efforts is crucial as we work together towards the NICE goals for a cybersecurity workforce that
meets the Nation's needs.

Appendix III: Comments from the Department of Defense

DEPARTMENT OF DEFENSE
6000 DEFENSE PENTAGON
WASHINGTON, D.C. 20301-6000

CHIEF INFORMATION OFFICER

NOV 1 4 2011

Mr. Gregory C. Wilshusen
Director, Information Security Issues
U.S. Government Accountability Office
441 G Street, NW
Washington, DC 20548

Dear Mr. Wilshusen:

In response to the attached GAO Draft Report, GAO-12-8, "CYBERSECURITY HUMAN CAPITAL: Initiatives Need Better Planning and Coordination," dated November 2011 (GAO Code 311062), the Department of Defense concurs with the first of the two recommendations. The progress the Department had made in workforce planning and competency development has been documented in the draft 2010 annual IT human capital plan to congress, which is pending final approval of the Under Secretary of Defense for Personnel and Readiness.

Regarding the second recommendation calling for an evaluation of the costs and benefits of the professional certification program, the Department does not concur; and based on subsequent communication, your office has agreed to omit this from the final report.

Additionally, we reviewed the report for accuracy and clarity of content, and have provided recommended changes.

The point of contact for this matter is Ms. Joyce France, at email: joyce.france@osd.mil, 571-372-4652.

Sincerely,

Teresa M. Takai

Attachment:
As stated

**GAO DRAFT REPORT DATED NOVEMBER 2011
GAO-12-8 (GAO CODE 311062)**

**"CYBERSECURITY HUMAN CAPITAL: INITIATIVES NEED
BETTER PLANNING AND COORDINATION"**

**DEPARTMENT OF DEFENSE COMMENTS
TO THE GAO RECOMMENDATIONS AND REPORT**

DOD COMMENTS TO THE RECOMMENDATIONS

RECOMMENDATION 1: The GAO recommends that the Secretary of Defense direct the
department's Chief Information Officer, in consultation with the Deputy Assistant Secretary for
Defense for Civilian Personnel Policy, update its department-wide cybersecurity workforce plan
or ensure that departmental components have plans that appropriately address human capital
approaches, critical skills, competencies, and supporting requirements for its cyber-security
workforce strategies. (See page 54/GAO Draft Report.)

DoD RESPONSE: Concur. The Department remains committed to the continual strengthening
and expansion of the workforce planning and competency development practices for its
cybersecurity personnel, as well the ongoing alignment of these practices to specific Component
skill and manning needs as they evolve. The progress that DoD has made towards the
achievement of this goal has been documented in the draft 2010 annual IT human capital plan to
Congress, which is pending final approval of the Under Secretary of Defense for Personnel and
Readiness.

Appendix IV: Comments from the Department of Health and Human Services

DEPARTMENT OF HEALTH & HUMAN SERVICES

OFFICE OF THE SECRETARY

Assistant Secretary for Legislation
Washington, DC 20201

Gregory C. Wilshusen, Director
Information Security Issues

OCT 24 2011

Valerie C. Melvin, Director
Information Management and Human Capital Issues

U.S. Government Accountability Office
441 G Street NW
Washington, DC 20548

Dear Mr. Wilshusen and Ms. Melvin:

Attached are comments on the U.S. Government Accountability Office's (GAO) draft report entitled, "CYBERSECURITY HUMAN CAPITAL: Initiatives Need Better Planning and Coordination" (GAO-12-8).

The Department appreciates the opportunity to review this report prior to publication.

Sincerely,

Jim R. Esquea
Assistant Secretary for Legislation

Attachment

**GENERAL COMMENTS OF THE DEPARTMENT OF HEALTH AND HUMAN
SERVICES (HHS) ON THE GOVERNMENT ACCOUNTABILITY OFFICE'S
(GAO) DRAFT REPORT ENTITLED, "CYBERSECURITY HUMAN CAPITAL:
INITIATIVES NEED BETTER PLANNING AND COORDINATION" (GAO-12-8)**

The Department appreciates the opportunity to review and comment on this draft report.

GAO Recommendation
*We recommend that the Secretary of Health and Human Services direct the department's
Chief Information Officer, in consultation with its Chief Human Capital Officer, to
develop and implement a departmentwide cybersecurity workforce plan or ensure that
departmental components are conducting appropriate workforce planning activities.*

HHS Response
Overall, we concur with the draft report's findings regarding our cybersecurity workforce
planning. The HHS Office of the Chief Information Officer (OCIO) will coordinate with
the Office of Human Resources to develop and implement a departmentwide
cybersecurity workforce plan, and ensure that departmental components are conducting
appropriate workforce planning activities. Target completion date is July 2012.

Appendix V: Comments from the Department of Homeland Security

U.S. Department of Homeland Security
Washington, DC 20528

November 10, 2011

Mr. Gregory C. Wilshusen
Director, Information Security Issues
U.S. Government Accountability Office
441 G Street, NW
Washington, DC 20548

Ms. Valerie C. Melvin
Director, Information Management and
Human Capital Issues
U.S. Government Accountability Office
441 G Street, NW
Washington, DC 20548

Re: Draft Report GAO-12-8, "CYBERSECURITY HUMAN CAPITAL: Initiatives Need Better Planning and Coordination"

Dear Mr. Wilshusen and Ms. Melvin:

Thank you for the opportunity to review and comment on this draft report. The U.S. Department of Homeland Security (DHS) appreciates the U.S. Government Accountability Office's (GAO's) work in planning and conducting its review and issuing this report.

The Department is pleased to note GAO's positive acknowledgement of actions DHS has taken to better define skills, competencies, roles, and responsibilities for the federal cybersecurity workforce. For example, the Department is working with the National Institute of Standards and Technology (NIST) and others to implement the National Initiative for Cybersecurity Education (NICE).

The Federal Government's goal for NICE is to establish an operational, sustainable, and continually improving cybersecurity education program that will enhance the Nation's security. Implementation of NICE requires coordination and collaboration between governments at all levels, industry, academia, non-government organizations, and the general public. NIST leads the overall NICE initiative, while DHS leads two of NICE's four components and co-leads a third.

The NICE program developed a Cybersecurity Workforce Framework (Framework), which identifies various cybersecurity workforce functions, or specialties. The Framework is an outgrowth of policy studies conducted by DHS, the Department of Defense and the Office of the Director of National Intelligence. Additionally, the Framework was socialized with more than 20 federal organizations, including the Federal Chief Information Officer Council, as well as partners in academia, industry, non-federal governments, and standardization and certification groups.

The Framework establishes 7 broad categories for cybersecurity work and 31 specific specialty areas, and identifies the functions, tasks, and aligned knowledge, as well as skill and ability requirements associated with these specialty areas. The Framework was recently posted for public comment to garner input from the widest possible workforce.

In June 2011, DHS sponsored a NICE Program Planning conference to review various projects that were already in the planning phases and designed to meet the goals and objectives defined in the NICE Strategic Plan. Work performed during this conference, and subsequent feedback received on the NICE Strategic Plan from the general public and federal partners, assisted DHS in gathering the information needed to create DHS's FY 2012 Program Plan for NICE Components 1, 3, and 4. These Program Plans are expected to be completed by the end of the first quarter of FY 2012 and coordinated within DHS and with other NICE partners early in the second quarter of FY 2012.

The draft report contains two recommendations directed at DHS, with which DHS concurs and has already initiated steps to implement. Specifically:

Recommendation 1: To ensure that government-wide cybersecurity workforce initiatives are better coordinated and planned, and to better assist federal agencies in defining roles, responsibilities, skills, and competencies for their workforce, GAO recommended that the Secretary of Commerce, Director of the Office of Management and Budget, Director of the Office of Personnel Management, and Secretary of Homeland Security:

- clarify the governance structure for NICE to specify responsibilities and processes for planning and monitoring of initiative activities;
- develop and finalize detailed plans allowing NICE to hold agencies accountable, measure progress, and determine resources to accomplish the activities they agree to undertake; and
- consolidate and align efforts to define roles, responsibilities, skills, and competencies for the federal cybersecurity workforce.

Response: Concur. DHS will coordinate with its NICE counterparts to document the existing governance structure, ensure a system for accountability, and define federal cybersecurity workforce roles, responsibilities, skills, and competencies. Specifically, DHS's NICE agency leads will develop NICE Component Plans that will be used to assess the progress achieved in addressing this recommendation to track business training, identify opportunities for improvement, and minimize duplication.

Recommendation 2: To ensure that the benefits of the training provided through the Information Systems Security Line of Business are maximized, and resources are used most efficiently, GAO recommended the Secretary of Homeland Security:

- implement a process for tracking agency use of line of business training and gathering feedback from agencies on the training's value and opportunities for improvement; and

2

- develop a process to coordinate training offered through the line of business to minimize the production and distribution of duplicative products.

Response: Concur. As clarification, the Information Systems Security Line's of Business (ISSLOB) is managed by the Office of Management and Budget, but aspects of the program are administered by DHS's National Cyber Security Division, Federal Network Security Branch. The role of ISSLOB is to provide cost avoidance services in support of securing federal networks. One of its initiatives focuses on providing federal agencies with training opportunities through Shared Service Centers (SSCs). The ISSLOB SSCs provide both Tier I mandatory generalized Security Awareness Training and Tier II optional Role-Based Training.

The DHS ISSLOB program is developing an SSC point of contact list for an annual data call for ISSLOB input for incorporation into future solutions to address this recommendation. ISSLOB will also work with the SSCs to ensure they have opportunities to align with the NICE activity and findings.

Again, thank you for the opportunity to review and comment on this draft report. Technical and sensitivity comments were previously provided under separate cover. We look forward to working with you on future Homeland Security issues.

Sincerely,

Jim H. Crumpacker
Director
Departmental GAO-OIG Liaison Office

3

Appendix VI: Comments from the Department of the Treasury

DEPARTMENT OF THE TREASURY
WASHINGTON, D.C. 20220

OCT 3 1 2011

Mr. Gregory C. Wilshusen
Director, Information Security Issues
U.S. Government Accountability Office
410 G Street, NW
Washington, DC 20548

Dear Mr. Wilshusen:

Thank you for your draft report on *"Cybersecurity Human Capital: Initiatives Need Better Planning and Coordination."* The Department appreciates the Government Accountability Office (GAO) recommendation to develop and implement a department-wide cyber security workforce plan or ensure that departmental components conduct appropriate workforce planning activities. The Treasury Department agrees with this recommendation.

In consultation with the Chief Human Capital Officer, the Office of the Chief Information Officer will ensure Departmental components are conducting appropriate workforce planning activities. Instructions will be issued to Treasury components with requirements to develop and submit plans to the Department for evaluation and feedback.

Thank you for your important efforts during this review. Please do not hesitate to contact me at 202-622-1200 should you have any questions.

Sincerely,

Robyn East
Deputy Assistant Secretary for Information Systems
and Chief Information Officer

Appendix VII: Comments from the Department of Veterans Affairs

DEPARTMENT OF VETERANS AFFAIRS
WASHINGTON DC 20420

November 1, 2011

Mr. Gregory C. Wilshusen
Director, Information Technology
U.S. Government Accountability Office
441 G Street, NW
Washington, DC 20548

Dear Mr. Wilshusen:

The Department of Veterans Affairs (VA) has reviewed the Government Accountability Office's (GAO) draft report, *CYBERSECURITY HUMAN CAPITAL: Initiatives Need Better Planning and Coordination* (GAO-12-8) and is providing comments in the enclosure.

VA appreciates the opportunity to comment on your draft report.

Sincerely,

John R. Gingrich
Chief of Staff

Enclosures

Enclosure

Department of Veterans Affairs (VA) Comments to
Government Accountability Office (GAO) Draft Report:
***CYBERSECURITY HUMAN CAPITAL: Initiatives Need Better
Planning and Coordination***
(GAO-12-8)

GAO Recommendation: **We recommend that the Secretary of Veterans Affairs direct the department's Chief Information Officer, in consultation with its Chief Human Capital Officer, to update its department-wide cybersecurity competency model or establish a cybersecurity workforce plan that fully addresses gaps in human capital approaches and critical skills and competencies, supporting requirements for its cybersecurity workforce strategies, and monitoring and evaluating agency progress.**

VA Response: Concur. The Chief Information Officer and the Chief Human Capital Officer will create and monitor an updated Department-wide cybersecurity workforce plan that fully addresses identified gaps in cybersecurity human capital; and approaches, critical skills, competencies, and support requirements for its cybersecurity workforce strategies.

VA recognizes the importance and value of a centralized cybersecurity workforce competency model. Development of a department-wide cybersecurity human capital workforce plan is necessary to achieve Chief Information Officers (CIO) Council guidelines. VA would welcome a standardized definition of what makes up the cybersecurity workforce to ensure we address the complete cybersecurity workforce.

Within VA's Office of Information and Technology (OIT), IT Workforce Development (ITWD) is working with Field Security Services, the Network Security Operations Center, and Service Delivery and Engineering to continue the development of competency models that effectively develop the essential skill sets of the cybersecurity workforce. Using the Federal CIO Council's "IT Roadmap of 2210 Parentheticals" as a guide to implementing competency models, the following areas will be developed: Application Software Developers, Customer Support, Data Management, Internet, Network Services, Operating Systems, Policy and Planning, Security, System Administration, System Analysis and Enterprise Architecture. ITWD will work to identify additional job functions requiring cybersecurity training based upon available data.

OIT will have competency models developed for the entire 2210 cybersecurity workforce by December 2012. Currently the GS 2210 cybersecurity workforce consists of Information Security Officers, Chief Information Officers and Network Security Operations Center staff as well as those who receive security role-based training such as Network, System and Database Administrators. These competency models will support the development of training identified by employee self-assessments and validated by supervisors to enhance the skills of the workforce. As additional job series are identified, ITWD will include additional job series as they are identified with specific role-based training until time and funding permits the development of competency models to improve the skills of the workforce.

1

Enclosure

Department of Veterans Affairs (VA) Comments to
Government Accountability Office (GAO) Draft Report:
CYBERSECURITY HUMAN CAPITAL: Initiatives Need Better
Planning and Coordination
(GAO-12-8)

OIT's current development plan includes:
- Security – implemented 2009 with additional technical competency developed 2011/2012
- Policy and Planning – CIOs implemented 2011
- Software Developers – implemented 2011
- OIT Core competency model – January 2012
- Supervisory model – January 2012
- Network Services – spring 2012
- System Administration – spring 2012
- Data Management – spring 2012
- IT Project/Program Management – spring 2012
- NSOC – Specifically identified areas, spring 2012, with specific profiles developed under the appropriate competency models as developed
- Customer Support – late summer 2012
- System Analysis – later summer 2012
- Internet – December 2012
- Operating Systems – December 2012
- Enterprise Architecture – December 2012

OIT will collaborate with Office of Chief Human Capital Officer to evaluate mandating the current or creating an updated internal certification program for cybersecurity professions and create a Department-wide cybersecurity staffing plan to competitively address alternative incentives.

Target Completion Date: January 30, 2013

2

Appendix VIII: Comments from the National Science Foundation

NATIONAL SCIENCE FOUNDATION
4201 WILSON BOULEVARD, Room 1270
ARLINGTON, VIRGINIA 22230

OFFICE OF THE
DIRECTOR

October 26, 2011

Mr. Gregory C. Wilshusen
Director, Information Security Issues
United States Government Accountability Office
Washington, DC 20548

Dear Mr. Wilshusen:

The National Science Foundation (NSF) appreciates the opportunity to review and comment on the Government Accountability Office's (GAO's) draft report entitled *Cybersecurity Human Capital: Initiatives Need Better Planning and Coordination (GAO-12-8)*. NSF commends the GAO team for its efforts to understand and capture the characteristics and features of the Scholarship for Service (SFS) program (pages 52-53) which is co-sponsored by NSF and DHS.

We are pleased that the report indicated that most of the agencies find the SFS program to be "a valuable resource for recruiting cybersecurity professionals." The report also noted that SFS "is a relatively small program..." We agree, but also wish to point out that increasing the number of SFS graduates will require more than providing additional scholarships.

In addition to the SFS program, NSF supports a number of activities that contribute ultimately to strengthening the U.S. cybersecurity workforce. We are currently exploring options on a number of fronts including helping to build the pipeline to cybersecurity careers in high schools and community colleges by mechanisms such as injecting cybersecurity topics into the new Computer Science AP courses; recruiting more women and underrepresented minorities to explore cybersecurity careers; and encouraging colleges and universities, including community colleges, to apply for National Centers of Academic Excellence in Information Assurance (CAE) designation.

NSF concurs that in the past information about how many students remain in federal service after their service repayment period has been fulfilled has been incomplete—largely due to the classified nature of a majority of the SFS positions. NSF agrees that tracking the retention rate is important. However, as drafted, the report's recommendation leaves the impression that this issue is not currently being addressed. That is not the case. We are in the process of implementing a new monitoring and evaluation system that will collect data from a variety of sources, including SFS employment data provided by the intelligence community directly to OPM. The new monitoring system will begin data collection in early 2012, and we will be able to provide the requested statistics starting in early FY 2013.

Thank you for the opportunity to comment on this draft report. If you have any questions regarding this response, please contact Kathryn Sullivan at 703-292-7375. We look forward to receiving your final report.

Sincerely,

Cora B. Marrett
Deputy Director

Appendix IX: Comments from the Office of Personnel Management

UNITED STATES OFFICE OF PERSONNEL MANAGEMENT
Washington, DC 20415

Employee Services

OCT 27 2011

Mr. Gregory C. Wilshusen
Director, Information Security Issues
441 G Street, NW., Room 4T21
Washington, DC 20548

Dear Mr. Wilshusen:

Thank you for providing the U.S. Office of Personnel Management (OPM) the opportunity to comment on the Government Accountability Office (GAO) draft report, "Cybersecurity Human Capital: Initiatives Need Better Planning and Coordination." We appreciate the opportunity to provide you with comments about this report.

Response to Recommendations

Recommendation: To help Federal agencies better identify their cybersecurity workforce, we recommend the Directors of OPM and the Office of Management and Budget (OMB) collaborate with the Chief Information Officer (CIO) Council to identify and develop Governmentwide strategies to address challenges Federal agencies face in tracking their cybersecurity workforce.

Management Response: We concur. Capturing data on the cybersecurity workforce will better enable agencies to identify, assess and develop strategies for their workforce. OPM will develop a data element for tracking the cybersecurity workforce in the Enterprise Human Resource Integration (EHRI) system, and we will collaborate with the CIO Council, OMB and other agencies as needed to implement.

Recommendation: To ensure that Governmentwide cybersecurity workforce initiatives are better coordinated and planned, and to better assist Federal agencies in defining roles, responsibilities, skills, and competencies for their workforce, we recommend that the Secretary of Commerce, Director of OMB, Director of OPM, and Secretary of Homeland Security:

- establish a clear governance structure for the National Initiative for Cybersecurity Education (NICE);
- develop and finalize detailed plans allowing NICE to hold agencies accountable, measure progress, and determine resources to accomplish its goals; and
- consolidate and align efforts to define roles, responsibilities, skills, and competencies for the Federal cybersecurity workforce.

We will address recommended actions separately.

www.opm.gov   Recruit, Retain and Honor a World-Class Workforce to Serve the American People   www.usajobs.gov

Mr. Gregory C. Wilshusen   2

Management Response:

- establish a clear governance structure for NICE; and
- develop and finalize detailed plans allowing NICE to hold agencies accountable, measure progress, and determine resources to accomplish its goals

We partially concur. While OPM is engaged in NICE as a subcomponent lead for the Federal Workforce Structure, the Director of OPM does not have authority to implement the recommendations involving NICE governance structure, accountability or resourcing. Recommend deletion of "Director of the Office of Personnel Management" from this action.

- consolidate and align efforts to define roles, responsibilities, skills, and competencies for the federal cybersecurity workforce.

We concur. OPM will continue to collaborate with officials and agencies involved in NICE and the CIO Council to ensure cybersecurity workforce efforts to define roles, responsibilities, skills and competencies are aligned and consolidated where possible.

Recommendation: To improve Governmentwide cybersecurity workforce planning efforts, we recommend the Director of OPM take the following actions:

- issue and finalize guidance to agencies on how to track the use and effectiveness of incentives for hard-to-fill positions, including cybersecurity positions; and
- maximize the value of the cybersecurity competency model by (1) developing and implementing a method for ensuring that the competency model accurately reflects the skill set unique to the cybersecurity workforce, (2) developing a method for collecting and tracking data on the use of the competency model, and (3) creating a schedule for revising or updating the model on a regular basis.

We will address recommended actions separately.

Management Response:

- issue and finalize guidance to agencies on how to track the use and effectiveness of incentives for hard-to-fill positions, including cybersecurity positions

We concur. The incentives that appear to be covered by this recommendation in GAO's draft report include recruitment, relocation, and retention incentives (3Rs), superior qualifications and special needs pay setting authority, scholarships, student employment programs, student loan repayments, and annual leave enhancements.

Mr. Gregory C. Wilshusen   3

With regard to the 3Rs, OPM is actively working with agencies and Shared Service Centers to
review 3Rs data reported to the EHRI system to better understand the data reported and revise
reporting requirements and system edits, as needed, so that the data can be used for OPM and
agency tracking and analysis. We also met with top 3Rs paying agencies to gain a better
understanding of how they track and measure 3Rs use. We found that some measured the
effectiveness of the 3Rs by their success in filling positions with highly qualified individuals or
the ability to retain employees in positions that without the incentives would be very difficult to
fill based on their past recruitment efforts. Others examined turnover rates, employee surveys,
rate of service agreement fulfillment, success of filling mission-critical positions and meeting
other staffing requirements (e.g., deployments or relocations), the cost of recruitment incentives
compared with the cost of attrition, production measures, management reports, and workforce
shaping results against technical and management needs. We plan to continue to work with
agencies to develop additional 3Rs guidance and share best practices.

Management Response:

- maximize the value of the cybersecurity competency model by (1) developing and
  implementing a method for ensuring that the competency model accurately reflects the
  skill set unique to the cybersecurity workforce, (2) developing a method for collecting
  and tracking data on the use of the competency model, and (3) creating a schedule for
  revising or updating the model on a regular basis.

We do not concur. (1) OPM used a job analysis methodology consistent with legal and
professional guidelines to ensure the accuracy of the competency model. (2) Use of OPM's
Governmentwide competency models is optional, to ensure agencies have the flexibility needed
to identify and address their own specific human capital needs. Additionally, we are working
with OMB to reduce agency human capital reporting requirements, rather than establishing new
requirements. (3) Consistent with legal and professional guidelines, OPM updates competency
models on an as-needed basis, rather than on an arbitrary timeline. Revising competency models
requires extensive input from subject matter experts across the Federal Government, pulling
them away from their critical work, and should only be done when the need outweighs the
resource cost.

Technical comments to the draft report are enclosed. Unless otherwise noted, the suggested
revisions are meant to provide technical accuracy.

Mr. Gregory C. Wilshusen   4

Please contact Ms. Janet Barnes, Deputy Director, Internal Oversight and Compliance on (202)
606-3270, should your office require additional information.

Again, my thanks to your office for providing this opportunity to update and clarify information
in the draft report.

Sincerely,

Angela Bailey
Associate Director
Employee Services

Enclosure

Appendix X: GAO Contacts and Staff Acknowledgments

GAO Contacts	Valerie C. Melvin, (202) 512-6304, or melvinv@gao.gov Gregory C. Wilshusen, (202) 512-6244, or wilshuseng@gao.gov
Staff Acknowledgments	In addition to the contacts named above, Vijay D'Souza (Assistant Director), Nancy Glover, Thomas Johnson, Tammi Kalugdan, Vernetta Marquis, Lee McCracken, Kate Nielsen, and Justin Palk made key contributions to this report.

www.ingramcontent.com/pod-product-compliance
Lightning Source LLC
Chambersburg PA
CBHW060456060326
40689CB00020B/4552